ELEMENTS of RELATIONAL DATABASE DESIGN

A Concise Presentation of Database Design from Initial Concepts through Normalization

David C. Hopkins

*Our mission is to efficiently provide the world's finest, most comprehensive
book publishing service, enabling every author to experience success.
To find out how to publish your book, your way, and have it available
worldwide, visit us online at www.trafford.com*

Trafford rev. 08/04/2010

North America & international
toll-free: 1 888 232 4444 (USA & Canada)
phone: 250 383 6864 ♦ fax: 812 355 4082

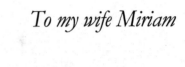

To my wife Miriam

Preface

This book was written with the intent of providing a concise presentation of the basic principles of database design. It deals with the widely accepted core definitions and conclusions that can be precisely stated and proven. Most of the topics covered are essential to the concluding chapter on "normalization" – a knowledge of which is crucial for avoiding problematic database designs.

In addition to brevity, the structure of the book is meant to minimize page turning by making it unnecessary to flip back to previous pages. For example, some definitions and results are repeated when referenced later. Also, with very few exceptions, examples are complete as they stand and don't refer to previous examples. To allow the reader to view all the information on a topic at once, the text appears on the left and the corresponding examples on the right of facing pages. Finally, to maintain the flow of the presentation, all proofs are in a separate appendix rather than in the main section of the book containing the various chapters.

By convention, statements labeled in boldface without any identifying numbers are definitions; that is, the word "Definition" is omitted. Statements labeled with the word "Theorem" in boldface with an identifying number are well known theorems usually associated with the originator. Statements with a boldface "Inference" number are also theorems but of lesser import than those labeled as a "Theorem." Algorithms are also identified in boldface with an associated number.

The book consists of five chapters as follows: The first two describe the basic techniques of modeling the real world with a database. Chapter Three covers common "operations" one can do with a database. Most of these operations pertain to using rather than designing a database; however, a few of them are also crucial for design. Chapter Four is dedicated to treating the various aspects of "dependency and decomposition" comprehensively in one place rather than introducing them piecemeal when they are needed for the various normal forms. The book concludes with Chapter Five's coverage of normalization where the various levels of good database design are defined along with procedures for attaining these levels. Also, problems that can occur when a database is not at a given level are described and illustrated by examples.

Table of Contents

Chapter 1
Modeling Entities

In this chapter we'll discuss how tables in a database are used to represent things (entities) from the real world. To be of use in a relational database, the tables must satisfy certain criteria; when they do they are called "relations." Relations are then shown to contain identifiers – called "keys" – by which data within the table can be located.

The definitions and conclusions comprising the remainder of this book follow as a matter of course from the few concepts presented here.

Section 1.1   Tables

We begin with a brief description of the means by which one creates and uses a relational database.

DBMS (Database Management System): The software that provides all the facilities for creating, modifying, interrogating and administering the database. Examples include Microsoft Access, SQL Server and Oracle.

SQL (Structured Query Language): The language used for all relational databases. The DBMS provides the SQL and though it is a standard language there are differences in it among the various DBMS's.

Note that some people pronounce SQL by saying each letter; while others pronounce it as the word "sequel." We'll use the former alternative and thus will write "an SQL statement" rather than "a SQL statement."

This book will not go further in discussing either DBMS's or SQL except to indicate in a general way the type of SQL commands used to implement the various concepts discussed. The actual SQL required will be somewhat dependent on the particular DBMS.

Relational Databases are comprised of a collection of tables. The remainder of this section contains definitions for the concepts relevant to the construction of a table.

Entity Instance: Something specific and uniquely distinguishable that we may wish to represent in a database.

Attribute: A named property of an entity instance that is of significance to the database; that is, the attribute name and its value for every entity instance of interest will be recorded in the database. An entity instance is uniquely identified by the values of all its attributes.

Atomic Value: A value for an attribute such that in the context of the database there is interest only in the whole value and not in any smaller component of it.

Domain: A pool of allowable values for an attribute. A domain should contain only atomic values.

Null: A special term used to indicate that an attribute value is either unknown or not applicable.

Entity Class: A generalization of an entity instance that represents a whole category of entity instances that have the same attributes.

Database design is largely concerned with attaining realistic and unproblematic representations of entity classes in the database. In the following, we define the database component – called a table – that is used to model an entity class because of its ability to represent any set of entity instances in the class.

Table:
1) Used to model an entity class by representing any set of its entity instances.
2) Usually named for the entity class that it models.
3) Consists of a header, rows and columns.
4) The attribute names appear above each column in the header. The attribute names are distinct; that is, no attribute name appears more than once.
5) Each column of the table contains the attribute values for various entity instances.
6) A row consists of values for each of the attributes and thus represents a specific entity instance.

A table is a "variable" in that it can have a different number of rows and different attribute values in the rows at different times.

In practice, tables are created and modified with the SQL statements CREATE TABLE and ALTER TABLE. Note that these statements deal with the table structure, not with the values in specific rows.

Example

To illustrate the concept of tables, consider a large company that's designing a company database. One of the things they want to model in the database is an entity class consisting of all the employees. An entity instance would be a specific employee. The properties of an employee that the company wishes to record in the database as attributes must be defined. The following chart is not part of the database, but is useful for defining and communicating the information to be included in the database table.

Attribute Name	Description	Domain
EmpID	The Employee's Company ID	Valid company Employee IDs
FirstName	First Name	Strings of 1-16 alphabetic characters
MI	Middle Initial	Strings of 1 alphabetic character
LastName	Last Name	Strings of 1-20 alphabetic characters
JobTitle	Job Title	Valid company Job Titles
OrgCode	Organization Code for the organization that an employee is assigned to within the company.	Valid company Organization Codes

Given the above information, we could use SQL to define the entity class to the DBMS as a table.

For communication purposes, we can denote the database table – which we'll call "Employees" – by Employees(ID, FirstName, MI, Lastname, JobTitle, OrgCode).

As mentioned, a table is a variable and can have different row values at different times. We can represent a "snapshot" of the table containing specific entity instances – that is, employees – as follows:

Employees

EmpID	FirstName	MI	LastName	JobTitle	OrgCode
E142	George	R	Fredericks	Senior Analyst	O3030
E013	John	Null	Robertson	HR Specialist	O1020
E184	Mary	L	Wilson	Analyst	O3030
E267	Ellen	K	Jefferson	Senior Programmer	O2000
E238	Henry	Null	Carter	Customer Representative	O4080
E197	Jane	E	Roosevelt	Senior Engineer	O2270
E058	Robert	A	Chesterton	HR Specialist	O1050
E189	Thomas	P	Browning	Section Chief	O0600

Section 1.2   Relations

Tables in a relational database must satisfy certain basic requirements; when these requirements are met, the table is said to be a "relation." The following definitions pertain to ensuring that a table is a relation.

Single Valued Attribute: An attribute that can only assume a single value from its domain – not a list of values.

Relation: A Table satisfying the following rules.

1) There is no order to the rows. That is, the table can be represented with the rows in any order without changing its meaning.
2) There is no order to the columns.
3) No two rows are the same. At least one attribute value must be different for any two rows.
4) All attributes are single valued. Namely, the value on any row for any column in the table is either the null value or a single value from that column's domain – not a list of values.

Note: The term "relation" comes from its similarity to a construct of the same name in mathematical set theory.

The preceding definition of a relation is all we need at this time; in Section 5.2 we'll discuss in detail how to obtain a relation from a table that doesn't satisfy condition 4.

The following concepts are pertinent to the further study of relations.

Predicate: A statement that gives the meaning of a relation by describing how the attributes are related to each other. The predicate should be true for the attribute values of each row in a relation.

As noted in Section 1.1, a table – and therefore a relation – is a variable because it can have a different number of rows and different attribute values in the rows at different times. We'll use the following definition to make a distinction between a relation and its value at a specific time.

Relation Occurrence: The value of a relation at some particular time with a specific number of rows and attribute values.

Note: We loosely use the term relation to refer to both relations and relation occurrences. When we discuss characteristics of a relation, we mean that the characteristics hold for all occurrences of the relation. On the other hand, examples generally use specific relation occurrences.

Example 1: Duplicate Rows

Suppose a large company wants to add a table called Emp to contain the company assigned job titles of each of its employees. If the attributes of the Emp table were First Name, Middle Initial, Last Name and the company Job Title for that employee, then the table could have values such as:

Emp

FirstName	MI	LastName	JobTitle
George	R	Fredericks	Senior Analyst
John	Null	Robertson	HR Specialist
Mary	*L*	*Wilson*	*Analyst*
Ellen	K	Jefferson	Senior Programmer
Mary	*L*	*Wilson*	*Analyst*
Thomas	P	Browning	Section Chief

The predicate for this simple table would be: The employee whose name is "FirstName, MI, Lastname" has the job title JobTitle.

As shown above, it's possible that there are two people with the same name and job title causing two rows to be the same. Thus the Emp table violates Rule 3) and is not a relation. One solution would be to add an attribute for unique employee IDs to produce the following table that is a relation:

Emp

EmpID	FirstName	MI	LastName	JobTitle
E142	George	R	Fredericks	Senior Analyst
E013	John	Null	Robertson	HR Specialist
E184	*Mary*	*L*	*Wilson*	*Analyst*
E267	Ellen	K	Jefferson	Senior Programmer
E058	*Mary*	*L*	*Wilson*	*Analyst*
E189	Thomas	P	Browning	Section Chief

Example 2: Non Single Valued Attribute

Let's assume that a company wants to design a relation called Emp/Proj that has all the projects on which each employee is working. The table will use the ID of each employee and the project ID of each active project. If the table has attributes EmpID and ProjID where ProjID is a list of all the projects that an employee is working on, then it could have values as follows:

Emp/Proj

EmpID	ProjID
E142	P12, P76
E013	P76
E184	P12, P20, P16

However, the Emp/Proj table is not a relation because the attribute values for the ProjID attribute are not all single valued and thus Rule 4 is violated. However, the following design is a relation:

Emp/Proj

EmpID	ProjID
E142	P12
E142	P76
E013	P76
E184	P12
E184	P20
E184	P16

Section 1.3　Keys

Since there's no order to the rows in a relation, it's necessary to have a way of identifying a row other than its position in the relation. As we'll see in this section, every relation always has a set of attributes that serves as a row identifier. Thus it turns out that rows can be uniquely identified by their contents.

This row identifier, generally called a key, is classified into three types – super key, candidate key and primary key – as follows:

Super Key: A set of attributes for a relation that has a different set of values in each row.

A super key serves as a row identifier. If we know the values for the set of attributes in a super key, we know the row in which those values occurred. That is, there is only one row with those values.

Since no two rows are the same in a relation, there always exists a super key – namely, the set of all the attributes.

Proper Subset: A subset that doesn't contain all the items in the original set.

Candidate Key: A super key for which no proper subset of its attributes is also a super key. Thus, it's a minimal super key; the term "candidate" reflects the fact that it may be chosen to be the Primary Key (defined next).

Primary Key: A candidate key chosen by the designer as the main row identifier for the relation.

Note: A primary key can be defined for the relation by using the SQL Create Table statement and the keyword "Primary Key" for the attributes that comprise the primary key (as appropriate for the DBMS being used).

Since the primary key is the principal means by which a row can be identified or found, we must ensure that it always has a meaningful value. Hence, there is a restriction or "constraint" on the values that a primary key can assume:

Entity Integrity Constraint: No attribute that is part of the primary key is ever allowed to be null.

Note: The entity integrity constraint can be explicitly specified for the relation by using the SQL Create Table statement and a keyword such as "Not Null" for the attributes that are part of the primary key.

We conclude this section with some additional terms concerning candidate keys.

Simple Candidate Key: A candidate key comprised of only one attribute.

Composite Candidate Key: A candidate key comprised of more than one attribute.

Overlapping Candidate Keys: Composite candidate keys that have one or more attributes in common.

Informational Attribute: An attribute that is not a candidate key and not part of one.

non-Key Attribute: An attribute that is not a candidate key (though it may be part of one).

Example 1: A Simple Candidate Key

For each row, the relation on the right gives the Job Title for the employee specified by the attribute EmpID that is a unique Employee ID. The only candidate key is the attribute EmpID. JobTitle is an informational attribute and therefore also a non-Key attribute.

Emp

EmpID	JobTitle
E14	Senior Analyst
E01	HR Specialist
E18	Analyst
E26	Senior Programmer
E23	Customer Representative
E19	Senior Engineer
E05	Analyst
E18	Section Chief

Example 2: A Composite Candidate Key

The attributes for the relation on the right consists of a unique company assigned Employee ID and a unique company assigned Project ID. The meaning of the relation is that for every row the employee whose ID equals the value of EmpID is assigned to the project whose ID equals the value of ProjID. For this relation the only super key, candidate key and primary key is the composite key consisting of the set of attributes {EmpID, ProjID}. There are no informational attributes; EmpID and ProjID are non-Key attributes.

Emp/Proj

EmpID	ProjID
E14	P12
E14	P76
E01	P76
E18	P12
E18	P20
E18	P16

Example 3: Overlapping Composite Candidate Keys

The attributes for the relation below consists of a unique Employee ID, a unique Project ID, a unique Project Name, and a number of Hours. The meaning of the relation is that for every row the employee worked a total of "Hours" hours on the project with ID "ProjID" whose project name is "ProjName." This relation has overlapping composite candidate keys {EmpID, ProjID} and {EmpID, ProjName}. Hours is an Informational Attribute; EmpID, ProjID and ProjName are non-Key attributes.

EmpID	ProjID	ProjName	Hours
E14	P12	Prepare Bid for Wilson Account	90
E14	P76	Replace Desktops in Engineering Department	20
E01	P76	Replace Desktops in Engineering Department	110
E18	P12	Prepare Bid for Wilson Account	75
E18	P20	Complete Five Year Plan	25
E18	P16	Develop Pricing for Product A	130

Chapter 2
Modeling Relationships

Thus far we have discussed the modeling of an entity class by a relation. However, there are often associations – called "relationships" – between entity classes that must also be modeled in the database. This chapter presents the concept of "Foreign Keys" that are used to model relationships followed by a discussion of "Referential Integrity" – a constraint on the values that may be assigned to a foreign key. Methods for using foreign keys to model the various types of relationships are presented as are the options for controlling how updates are handled to maintain referential integrity.

Section 2.1 Foreign Keys

First we formalize the rather intuitive notion of when sets of attribute values are considered equal.

Equality of Values of Attribute Sets: Let A be a set of attributes from a relation R and B an equal number of attributes from a relation S (not necessarily distinct from R) such that each attribute in A corresponds to an attribute in B and has the same domain. If r is a row in R and s is a row in S where the value for each attribute in A equals the value of the corresponding attribute in B, then we say that the value of A in row r equals the value of B in row s.

Next, we present a means by which each row in a relation can be associated with a row in another relation.

Foreign Key: Let Fkey be a set of attributes in some relation F and Ckey be a candidate key in some relation C. If the value of Fkey on each row of F always equals the value of Ckey in some row of C, then we say that Fkey is a foreign key in F that references Ckey in C. (Note that F and C aren't necessarily distinct.)

Terminology: Given the naming in the preceding definition, we say that relation F **references** relation C.

Notation: **F→C** means that relation F references relation C. That is, F contains the foreign key and C contains the referenced candidate key.

Referencing Relation: The relation containing the foreign key that references a candidate key in another relation.

Referenced Relation: The relation containing the candidate key that is referenced by the foreign key in another relation.

Target Relation: Another name for the referenced relation.

Self Referencing Relation: A relation that references itself. That is, the foreign key and the referenced candidate key are in the same relation with, of course, different attribute names.

Inherent to foreign keys is a restriction on their allowable values as specified in the following.

Referential Integrity Constraint: Every foreign key value must match one of the referenced candidate key values in the referenced relation or be null.

Note: Referential Integrity could be implemented for a given foreign key by using the SQL Create Table or Alter Table statements with the appropriate keyword such as "references" to declare the foreign key and the referenced relation. This will instruct the database to accept only valid foreign key values; that is, values that either equal the referenced candidate key in some row of the referenced relation or are null. (This assumes that the candidate key is the primary key in the referenced relation.)

Example 1: Referenced Relation Different from Referencing Relation

The attributes for the relation on the right consists of a unique company assigned Employee ID and a unique company assigned Project ID. For every row, the employee whose ID equals the value of EmpID is assigned to the project whose ID equals the value of ProjID. Individuals can be assigned to more than one project. The ProjID attribute serves as an example of a foreign key referencing the candidate key ProjID attribute in the Projects relation presented below.

Emp/Proj

EmpID	ProjID
E14	P12
E14	P76
E01	P76
E18	P12
E18	P20
E18	P16

(Foreign Key)

Proj

In the Proj relation presented to the right, attribute ProjID is a candidate key that is referenced by the foreign key ProjID in the Emp/Proj relation.

Thus we have Emp/Proj→Proj.

ProjID	ProjName
P12	Prepare Bid for Wilson Account
P76	Replace Desktops in Engineering Department
P20	Complete Five Year Plan
P16	Develop Pricing for Product A

Example 2: A Self-Referencing Relation

Emp

An employee with EmpID has the specified JobTitle and his/her immediate supervisor's ID is SupID. SupID is a foreign key that references the candidate key EmpID.

In this case, we have Emp→Emp.

EmpID	JobTitle	SupID
E14	Senior Analyst	E18
E01	HR Specialist	E20
E23	Customer Representative	E20
E19	Senior Engineer	E18
E18	Supervisor Level 2	E24
E24	Supervisor Level 1	E12
E12	Company President	Null
E20	Supervisor Level 2	E24

(Foreign Key)

Section 2.2 Relationships

As discussed in Chapter 1, entity classes are modeled with relations. To complete our database model, there is another aspect of the real world to consider: associations between entity classes.

Entity Class Relationships: It often happens that every entity instance of an entity class is associated with some number of entity instances in another – not necessarily different – entity class. When this happens, we say that there is a relationship between the two entity classes.

Cardinality of a Relationship: Cardinality refers to the number of entity instances of each entity class that are associated. The number is not specific: we only distinguish between one and "many" where many means "one or more." For entities F and G the possible cardinalities are 1 to 1, Many to 1, and Many to Many as follows:

<u>1 to 1</u>: 1 instance of F can be associated with at most 1 instance of G; 1 instance of G can be associated with at most 1 instance of F.
<u>Many to 1</u>: 1 instance of F can be associated with at most 1 instance of G; 1 instance of G can be associated with many instances of F.
<u>Many to Many</u>: 1 instance of F can be associated with many instances of G; 1 instance of G can be associated with many instances of F.

Optionality of a Relationship: Each entity class in a relationship has an optionality of either "mandatory" or "optional." Mandatory means that each instance of that entity class must "participate" in the relationship; that is, each instance must be associated with at least one instance in the other entity class. Optional means that each instance may or may not participate in the relationship.

In the database model, entity instances of an entity class are represented by rows in a relation. Hence, in the database, cardinality of a relationship refers to the number of rows in each relation that are associated. Optionality refers to whether or not each row in a relation must be associated with at least one row in the other relation.

In Section 2.1, we discussed how a foreign key is used to establish an association between rows in two relations. The fact that rows in a relation represent entity instances in an entity class suggests that foreign keys can be useful for modeling relationships.

<u>Modeling Entity Class Relationships:</u>

Below, we present approaches for modeling three common types of relationships.

In the following, let F and G be entity classes where R_F and R_G are the relations that model them.

Case 1: A 1 to 1 relationship with R_F mandatory and R_G optional. Each row in R_F matches exactly one row in R_G; a row in R_G may match one row in R_F. To model this case, define a candidate key from R_G as a foreign key in R_F to form $R_F{\rightarrow}R_G$ and specify that the value of this foreign key is NOT Null.

Case 2: A Many to 1 Relationship with R_F mandatory and R_G optional: Each row in R_F must match exactly one row in R_G; each row in R_G may match many rows in R_F. As in Case 1, assigning a candidate key from R_G as a non-Null foreign key in R_F to get $R_F{\rightarrow}R_G$ can model this case.

Case 3: A Many to Many Relationship with R_F optional and R_G optional: Each row in R_F may match many rows in R_G; each row in R_G may match many rows in R_F. This case can't be modeled by just adding foreign keys to R_F or R_G. However, we can use the following method to obtain a model of this case.

1) Add an "intermediate" relation R_{FG} with attributes consisting of candidate keys from R_F and R_G. The only candidate key for this new relation is the set of all its attributes.
2) Define the candidate key for R_F as a foreign key in R_{FG} referencing R_F and the candidate key for R_G as a foreign key in R_{FG} referencing R_G.

Thus the Many to Many relationship is replaced by the Many to 1 relationships $R_{FG} {\rightarrow} R_F$ and $R_{FG} {\rightarrow} R_G$.

In Chapter 3, we'll see that the various "Join" operators can be used to combine the associated rows of relations that model relationships with a foreign key.

Example 1: A 1 to 1 Relationship with Optional and Mandatory Relations

The relation Emp below gives the job title for the employee with the specified ID. Some of the employees have the additional duty of being a Safety Monitor as modeled in the relation Monitor that gives the ID of each safety monitor and the date he/she was certified. There's a 1 to 1 relationship between the two relations. Emp is Optional because not every row participates in the relationship; Monitor is Mandatory because every row must be associated with a row in Emp.

This relationship can be modeled by defining the EmpID attribute in Monitor as a foreign key referencing the EmpID attribute in Emp to get Monitor→Emp. EmpID is a primary key in Monitor and thus non-Null.

Emp

EmpID	JobTitle
E01	HR Specialist
E14	Analyst
E23	Accountant
E19	Engineer

Monitor

EmpID	CertDate
E01	1/1/2006
E14	7/5/2008

(Foreign key)

Example 2: A Many to 1 Relationship with Optional and Mandatory Relations

For every row in relation Emp/Proj below the employee with the specified ID is assigned to the project with ProjID. Individuals can be assigned to more than one project. The relation Proj gives the Project Name for every Project ID. Since a row in Proj can be associated with more than one row in Emp/Proj, there's a Many to 1 relationship between Emp/Proj and Proj. Because every row in Emp/Proj must be associated with a row in Proj, Emp/Proj is Mandatory in the relationship. However, a project may have no one assigned and, thus, Proj is optional.

This Many to 1 relationship can be modeled by defining the ProjID attribute in Emp/Proj as a non-Null foreign key referencing the ProjID attribute in Proj to get Emp/Proj→Proj.

Proj

ProjID	ProjName
P12	Prepare Bid
P76	Five Year Plan
P20	Develop Pricing
P45	Set Up Branch

Emp/Proj

EmpID	ProjID
E14	P12
E14	P76
E01	P76

(Foreign key)

Example 3: Modeling a Many to Many Relationship with Two Many to 1 Relationships

Consider the foregoing relations Emp and Proj. The employee represented on any row of Emp could be involved in many projects represented by rows in Proj. Also, every project on a row in Proj could involve many employees represented by rows in Emp. Thus there is a Many to Many relationship between the relations Emp and Proj.

We've seen in Example 2 that there's a Many to 1 relationship between Emp/Proj and Proj with ProjID a foreign key in Emp/Proj. Similarly, one could show that there's a Many to 1 relationship between Emp/Proj and Emp with EmpID a foreign key in Emp/Proj. Thus, Emp/Proj is suitable as an intermediate relation to model the Many to Many relationship between Emp and Proj by using the two Many to 1 relationships Emp/Proj→Emp and Emp/Proj→Proj.

For example, row (P76, Five Year Plan) in Proj is associated with rows (E14, P76) and (E01, P76) in Emp/Proj, which in turn is associated with rows (E14, Analyst), (E01, HR Specialist) in Emp. Thus a row in Proj is associated with two rows in Emp.

In a like manner the row (E14, Analyst) in Emp is associated (through Emp/Proj) with the rows (P12, Prepare Bid) and (P76, Five Year Plan) in Proj.

In this way, we obtain a model of the Many to Many relationship between Emp and Proj.

Section 2.3 Foreign Key Update Rules

In this section we present some options that enable the database designer to control how the DBMS should handle updates and deletes that would cause a violation of referential integrity.

Update considerations for foreign keys:

Assume we have implemented referential integrity for a foreign key by defining it and the referenced relation and candidate key to the DBMS using the appropriate SQL statements and keywords. We are then assured that only valid foreign key values will be accepted. This means that not only will invalid foreign key values be rejected but updates to the referenced relation will also be rejected if they would cause an invalid foreign key.

For example, if we try to delete a row in the referenced relation whose referenced candidate key value equals a foreign key value in the referencing relation, the delete will be rejected. This is because the deletion would cause the foreign key value to not match any of the candidate key values in the referenced relation and, therefore, to become invalid. Similarly, an attempt to alter the value of the candidate key in a referenced relation that equals a foreign key value in a referencing relation will be rejected.

The foregoing "default" actions may be how the database designer wants updates to the referenced relation for a particular database to be handled. However, there are other SQL features that allow the designer to change these referential integrity actions. These features are "delete cascade" and "update cascade." The keywords, which vary for different DBMS's, can be specified with the SQL Create Table or Alter Table statements.

Foreign Key options for deleting rows and updating primary keys in a referenced relation: One may choose one of the following delete options and one update option for a given foreign key and referenced relation:

Default for Delete (no option specified): Delete only those rows in the referenced relation whose candidate key value doesn't equal any foreign key value in the referencing relation.

Delete Cascade: Delete the row in the referenced relation and also delete all rows in the referencing relation whose foreign key value equals the candidate key value in the deleted row.

Default for update (no option specified): Update only those candidate key values in the referenced relation that don't equal any foreign key value in the referencing relation.

Update Cascade: Update the candidate key value in the referenced relation and also update all foreign key values that equal the old candidate key value to the new candidate key value in the referencing relation.

Examples: Foreign Key Update Rules

The ProjID attribute for the Emp/Proj relation below is a foreign key that references the candidate key ProjID in the Proj relation. Assume that these relations have initial values as indicated.

Emp/Proj			Proj	
EmpID	ProjID		ProjID	ProjName
E14	P12		P12	Prepare Bid
E14	P76		P76	Five Year Plan
E01	P76		P20	Develop Pricing
	(Foreign key)		P45	Set Up Branch

Case 1. The Default for Delete is in force. That is, Delete Cascade hasn't been specified. Then an attempt to delete the row in the Proj relation with ProjID value P76 will fail because this delete would cause the rows in the Emp/Proj relation with values {E14, P76} and {E01, P76} to violate referential integrity. That is, the foreign key values wouldn't match any values of ProjID in Proj.

Case 2. Delete Cascade has been specified. Then the deletion of the row in the Proj relation with ProjID value P76 will result in the values shown below.

Emp/Proj			Proj	
EmpID	ProjID		ProjID	ProjName
E14	P12		P12	Prepare Bid
			P20	Develop Pricing
			P45	Set Up Branch

Case 3. The Default for Update is in force. That is, Update Cascade hasn't been specified. Then – using the initial values for the relations – an attempt to update the value of ProjID in the Proj relation from P76 to P77 will fail because this change would cause the rows in the Emp/Proj relation with values {E14, P76} and {E01, P76} to violate referential integrity. That is, the foreign key values wouldn't match any values of ProjID in Proj.

Case 4. Update Cascade has been specified. Then – using the initial values for the relations – changing the value of ProjID in the Proj relation from P76 to P77 will result in the values shown below.

Emp/Proj			Proj	
EmpID	ProjID		ProjID	ProjName
E14	P12		P12	Prepare Bid
E14	P77		P77	Five Year Plan
E01	P77		P20	Develop Pricing
			P45	Set Up Branch

Chapter 3
Relational Algebra

In the previous chapters, we've discussed using relations and foreign keys to construct a database that accurately models real world entities and the relationships among them. Subsequent chapters will be concerned with refining the relations to minimize problems. In this chapter, we'll suspend our discussion of database design as we look at the database from the user's point of view by presenting some of the operations for manipulating the data in the database. Additionally, two of these operations – "project" and "natural join" – will be needed when we return to the discussion of database design in the chapters that follow.

Relational Operators: Functions that are applied to one or two input relations to produce a single output relation – also called the result relation. These operators can be implemented with SQL to enable one to extract information for reports or other purposes.

The result of a relational operation must be a relation and thus includes not only the contents of the rows but also the header consisting of the attribute names. Hence, we'll follow Darwen's approach [Wa] and pay particular attention to the attribute names of both the input and result relations in our definitions.

Notation for these operators is not particularly standardized; at the cost of some conciseness we'll use notation that is self-explanatory and avoids the use of special characters.

Some of the relational operators are, in a sense, more fundamental than others. We begin by defining some terms pertaining to this concept.

Primitive: An operator is primitive if its result can't be duplicated by a sequence of other operators.

Definable: A relational operator is definable if it is not primitive. That is, there is a sequence of other operations that produce the same result. We say that the operator is defined by this sequence.

Of the nine operators we'll discuss, six are primitive: RENAME, SELECT, PROJECT, UNION, DIFFERENCE and PRODUCT. The remaining three - INTERSECT, the various JOIN operators, and DIVIDE - are definable in terms of the primitive operators.

Unary, **Binary**: Unary operators use just a single input relation to produce a result relation; Binary operators produce a result relation from two input relations.

Section 3.1 Unary Operators: Rename, Select and Project

Rename: Given a relation, construct a new relation that has different names for some of the attributes in the original. The heading will consist of the unchanged attribute names and the new names for those changed. The rows will be the same as the original with values for the changed attribute names in the column for the corresponding new name.

For a relation, R, with some subset of attributes {A1, …AN}, we'll use the following expression to represent the relation resulting from the renaming of the attributes of R from A1 to A1new, … AN to ANnew.

RENAME (R, A1 to A1new, … AN to ANnew)

Implementing RENAME in SQL: Use the SQL select statement with the keyword "AS."

Select: Given a relation, construct a new relation that only contains certain rows from the original. The heading (attribute names) will be the same as for the original relation and the rows will be those for which some "condition expression" involving the relation's attributes is TRUE for the attribute values on that row. (Note that the select operator should not be confused with the SQL select statement).

Comparison Condition for Select: For any relation, R, a comparison condition, C_R, is an expression containing attribute names and comparison operators ($=, \neq, >, <, \leq, \geq$) that evaluates to TRUE, FALSE or UNKNOWN for the attribute values on any row.

The expression may also contain constants and other operators: logical (AND, OR, NOT) and arithmetic ($+, -, *, /$). Parenthesis may be used to clarify the evaluation order.

In addition to TRUE or FALSE, the value of C_R could be UNKNOWN for a given row because one of the attributes values for that row could be Null. Only rows for which C_R is TRUE – not FALSE or UNKNOWN – will be selected.

The following expression represents the result relation from the selection from R subject to condition C_R:
SEL (R, C_R)

Implementing SEL in SQL: Use the SQL select statement and the "WHERE" clause.

Example 1: Rename

Suppose we have the following relation with the indicated attribute values where YearEx is the amount that the employee has spent entertaining customers in the current year and MaxEx is the amount that the employee is authorized to spend in the current year:

Employees

EmployeeID	LastName	Gender	JobTitle	YearEx	MaxEx
E14	Fredericks	M	Senior Engineer	50	400
E01	Robertson	M	HR Specialist	525	1000
E17	Wilson	F	Analyst	0	150
E23	Carter	M	Customer Rep	1800	2000
E19	Roosevelt	F	Senior Engineer	650	500
E18	Browning	M	Section Chief	1630	1500
E06	Masters	F	Senior Engineer	80	300

The result of performing the following RENAME operation appears below.

RENAME (Employees, EmployeeID to EmpID, LastName to LName)

Employees

EmpID	LName	Gender	JobTitle	YearEx	MaxEx
E14	Fredericks	M	Senior Engineer	50	400
E01	Robertson	M	HR Specialist	525	1000
E17	Wilson	F	Analyst	0	150
E23	Carter	M	Customer Rep	1800	2000
E19	Roosevelt	F	Senior Engineer	650	500
E18	Browning	M	Section Chief	1630	1500
E06	Masters	F	Senior Engineer	80	300

Example 2: Select by Comparing Attribute Values to Constants

The result of performing the following SELECT operation on the original relation appears below.
SEL (Employees, "Gender = 'F' AND JobTitle = 'Senior Engineer' ")

EmployeeID	LastName	Gender	JobTitle	YearEx	MaxEx
E19	Roosevelt	F	Senior Engineer	650	500
E06	Masters	F	Senior Engineer	80	300

Example 3: Select by Comparing Two Attribute Values

The result of performing the following SELECT operation on the original relation appears below.
SEL (Employees, "YearEx > MaxEx")

EmployeeID	LastName	Gender	JobTitle	YearEx	MaxEx
E19	Roosevelt	F	Senior Engineer	650	500
E18	Browning	M	Section Chief	1630	1500

Project: Given a relation, construct a new relation that only contains columns for some specified attributes from the original. The new relation will have a header comprised of the specified attribute names. A row will appear in the resulting relation if and only if the attribute values on that row appeared together on a row in the original relation. Also – to ensure that the result is a relation – duplicate rows will be eliminated.

Let ASET be a subset of the attributes of a relation, R. Then we'll represent the relation resulting from the projection of R on ASET by the following expression.

PROJECT (R, ASET)

We'll use the symbol "$\cup$" to mean the normal set union. Thus if $A_1, ... A_n$ are subsets of the attributes of a relation R, then $A_1 \cup ... A_n$ represents the set union of these subsets; that is, it's the set of all the attributes that are in at least one of the subsets $A_1, ... A_n$. Thus, the projection on all the attributes in $A_1, ... A_n$ will be written as:

PROJECT (R, $A_1 \cup ... A_n$)

Also, if $A_1, ... A_n$ are attributes – rather than sets of attributes – we could write PROJECT (R, $\{A_1, ... A_n\}$).

Implementing PROJECT in SQL: Use the SQL select statement and specify the columns to be included.

Section 3.2 Simple Binary Operators: Union, Difference and Intersect

The remaining operators to be presented are all binary; that is, they use two input relations to produce a new result relation. They will be represented by expressions of the form R OPER S, where R and S are the input relations and OPER is the name of the operation. There are three properties – commutivity, associativity and distributivity– that can be useful when dealing with these types of operators. Some of the operators have these properties and some don't.

Commutivity: Let OPER be an operation and R and S be relations. Then OPER is said to be commutative if R OPER S = S OPER R

Associativity: Let OPER be an operation and R, S, and T be relations. Then OPER is said to be associative if R OPER (S OPER T) = (R OPER S) OPER T

Distributivity: Let OPER1 and OPER2 be two binary operations; Let R, S and T be relations. Then OPER1 is said to be distributive over OPER2 if R OPER1 (S OPER2 T) = (R OPER1 S) OPER2 (R OPER1 T)

The next three operators that we'll discuss – UNION, MINUS, and INTERSECT – require a specific type of similarity between the input relations called union compatibility.

Union Compatible: Two relations are said to be union compatible if they have the same number of attributes, the same attribute names, and the same domain for attributes that have the same name.

Union: Given two union compatible relations, construct a new relation that contains all the rows from the two original relations. The new relation will have a header comprised of the attribute names that each of the original relations have. A row will appear in the new relation if and only if the row also appeared in either of the original relations. Further – to ensure that the result is a relation – duplicate rows will be eliminated.

The following expression will represent the union of any two union compatible relations R and S.

R UNION S

<u>Union Properties</u>: UNION is both commutative and associative. Hence, for union compatible relations R, S, and T:

R UNION S = S UNION R
R UNION (S UNION T) = (R UNION S) UNION T

Implementing UNION in SQL: Connect SQL select statements with the "UNION" operator.

Example 1: Project

The relation Achieve below lists the employee ID, gender and job title of employees who've received a special achievement award in the current year. To its right, the result of forming the projection of Achieve on the attribute set {Gen, JobTitle} appears. The italicized rows would lead to duplicate rows in the projection if not for the requirement that duplicate rows are eliminated.

Achieve

EmpID	Gen	JobTitle
E14	M	Engineer
E01	M	HRSpecialist
E18	*F*	*Programmer*
E26	*F*	*Programmer*
E19	*F*	*Engineer*
E23	M	Customer Rep
E06	*F*	*Engineer*

Project(Achieve, {Gen, JobTitle})

Gen	JobTitle
M	Engineer
M	HRSpecialist
F	Programmer
F	Engineer
M	Customer Rep

Example 2: UNION

The relation Service below lists employees who've received a community service award for the current year. Service is union compatible with Achieve. To the right the union of Service and Achieve appears. The italicized rows exist in both Service and Achieve (above) and illustrate that duplicate rows are eliminated in the UNION.

Service

EmpID	Gen	JobTitle
E01	*M*	*HRSpecialist*
E09	M	Accountant
E23	*M*	*Customer Rep*
E10	M	Analyst

Service UNION Achieve

EmpID	Gen	JobTitle
E14	M	Engineer
E01	M	HRSpecialist
E18	F	Programmer
E26	F	Programmer
E19	F	Engineer
E23	M	Customer Rep
E06	F	Engineer
E09	M	Accountant
E10	M	Analyst

— Section 3.1: Project, Section 3.2: Union —

Difference: Given two union compatible relations in some order, construct a new relation that contains all the rows that are in the first relation but not in the second. The new relation will have a header comprised of the attribute names in each of the original relations.

The following expression represents the difference for any two union compatible relations R and S.

R MINUS S

Difference Properties: MINUS is not commutative and not associative. It's not distributive over UNION in the usual left to right sense, but is distributive "from the right." That is:
R MINUS (S UNION T) doesn't always equal (R MINUS S) UNION (R MINUS T).
However, (R UNION S) MINUS T = (R MINUS T) UNION (S MINUS T).

Implementing DIFFERENCE in SQL: Connect SQL select statements with operators such as EXCEPT or MINUS. As usual, different methods may be needed for the DBMS being used.

Intersection: Given two union compatible relations, construct a new relation that contains all the rows that are in both of the two original relations. That is, a row will appear in the new relation if and only if the row appeared in each of the original relations. The new relation will have a header comprised of the attribute names that are in each of the original relations.

The following expression represents the intersection of any two union compatible relations R and S.

R INTERSECT S

Intersect Properties: INTERSECT is commutative, associative and distributive over UNION. If R, S, and T are union compatible relations then:

R INTERSECT S = S INTERSECT R
R INTERSECT (S INTERSECT T) = (R INTERSECT S) INTERSECT T
R INTERSECT (S UNION T) = (R INTERSECT S) UNION (R INTERSECT T)

Also, INTERSECT is not a primary operation; it is definable from MINUS as follows:

R INTERSECT S = R MINUS(R MINUS S)

To implement an INTERSECT in SQL: Connect SQL select statements with the "INTERSECT" operator. Also, since INTERSECT is not primary, it is possible to define it from the implementation of MINUS.

Example 1: Difference

The relation DomesticProducts contains the product number and product name for all the products that some company manufactures domestically.

DomesticProducts

ProdNum	Name
P01	Rotor
P15	Pad
P18	Brake Cylinder
P07	Fluid Line
P20	Master Cylinder
P10	Hardware Kit

The relation ForeignProducts contains the product number and product name for all the products that some company manufactures in a foreign country.

ForeignProducts

ProdNum	Name
P19	Ball Joint
P02	Tie Rod End
P18	Brake Cylinder
P23	Master Cylinder
P20	Caliper

The result of performing the operation DomesticProduct MINUS ForeignProducts appears to the right. This relation will contain those products that are only manufactured domestically.

ProdNum	Name
P01	Rotor
P15	Pad
P07	Fluid Line
P10	Hardware Kit

Example 2: Intersection

The result of performing the operation DomesticProduct Intersect ForeignProducts appears to the right. This relation will contain those products that are manufactured domestically and in foreign countries.

ProdNum	Name
P18	Brake Cylinder
P23	Master Cylinder

Section 3.3 Concatenation Operators: Product, Join(s) and Divide

Concatenation: We'll use this term to describe the combining of a row from one input relation with a row from another. That is, if $r_1, \ldots r_m$ are the attribute values for some row in a relation R and $s_1, \ldots s_n$ are the attribute values for some row in a relation S, then the concatenation of these rows is $r_1, \ldots r_m, s_1, \ldots s_n$.

Product: Given two relations with no common attribute names, construct a new relation by concatenating each row of one relation with each row of the other. The heading will be comprised of all the attribute names of both input relations. The requirement that no attribute name appears in both input relations ensures that none are repeated in the new heading. One could use the RENAME operator to change attribute names to meet this requirement before forming the product. A convenient renaming practice is to prefix the attribute name by the relation name and a period.

Let R be a relation with attribute names $R_1, \ldots R_m$ and S be a relation with attribute names $S_1, \ldots S_n$ with no common attribute names between R and S. Then the attribute values $r_1, \ldots r_m, s_1, \ldots s_n$ form a row in the result relation with each r_i in the column for R_i and each s_i in the column for S_i if and only if:

1) $r_1, \ldots r_m$ form a row in R with each r_i in the column for R_i

AND 2) $s_1, \ldots s_n$ form a row in S with each s_i in the column for S_i.

The following expression represents the product of any two relations R and S.

R TIMES S

Product Properties: TIMES is both commutative and associative and is distributive over UNION.

Thus, if R, S, and T are relations with no common attribute names, then the following hold:

Commutivity: R TIMES S = S TIMES R
Associativity: R TIMES (S TIMES T) = (R TIMES S) TIMES T

Let R and S be relations with no common attribute names; let S and T be UNION compatible. Then we have:

Distributivity over UNION: R TIMES (S UNION T) = (R TIMES S) UNION (R TIMES T)

The number of columns in the product is equal to the sum of the number of columns in each of the input relations. The number of rows is equal to the product of the number of rows in each relation.

Implementing PRODUCT in SQL: Specify the tables in the "FROM" clause of an SQL select statement.

In practice, various Joins as discussed below – rather than the product – are usually used to combine the rows of relations.

Example: Product

A manufacturer of refrigerators offers a model for any choice of freezer location, size and color. The available freezer locations are specified in the relation to the right.

FreezerLocation

FreezerLocation
Top
Bottom
Left Side
Right Side

The available sizes in cubic feet appear in the Size relation.

Size

Size
14.5
18.5
22

The available colors appear in the Colors relation.

Colors

Colors
White
Black

The available combinations of freezer location, size and color are contained in the relation resulting from FreezerLocation TIMES Size TIMES Color as in the relation to the right.

Freezer Location	Size	Color
Top	14.5	White
Bottom	14.5	White
Left Side	14.5	White
Right Side	14.5	White
Top	18.5	White
Bottom	18.5	White
Left Side	18.5	White
Right Side	18.5	White
Top	22	White
Bottom	22	White
Left Side	22	White
Right Side	22	White
Top	14.5	Black
Bottom	14.5	Black
Left Side	14.5	Black
Right Side	14.5	Black
Top	18.5	Black
Bottom	18.5	Black
Left Side	18.5	Black
Right Side	18.5	Black
Top	22	Black
Bottom	22	Black
Left Side	22	Black
Right Side	22	Black

Joins: A group of operators that entails concatenating certain rows from two input relations to form a result relation. There are two classes of joins: inner joins and outer joins. When the type of join isn't specified, we assume it's the inner join.

Inner Joins: The types of Inner Joins are Theta-Join, Equi-Join, and Natural Join.

θ-Join (Theta-Join): Given two relations with no common attribute names, construct a new relation by concatenating those pairs of rows – one from each relation – that satisfy a comparison condition on the attribute values in the row from the first relation to the values in the row from the second. The RENAME operator can be used to ensure that there are no common attribute names before doing the θ-Join. The heading will be comprised of all the attribute names of both input relations.

For relations R and S with no attribute names in common, we describe the comparison condition much as we did for the Select operator except that now two relations are involved.

Comparison Condition for θ-Join: A comparison condition $C_{R,S}$ is an expression containing attribute names from relations R and S and comparison operators ($=$, $\neq$, $>$, $<$, $\leq$, $\geq$) that evaluates to TRUE, FALSE or UNKNOWN for the attribute values on any pair of rows – one from R and one from S.

The expression may also contain constants and other operators: logical (AND, OR, NOT) and arithmetic ($+, -, *, /$). Parenthesis may be used to clarify the evaluation order.

In addition to TRUE or FALSE, the value of $C_{R,S}$ could be UNKNOWN for a given pair of rows because one of the attributes values could be Null. Only pairs of rows for which $C_{R,S}$ is TRUE – not FALSE or UNKNOWN – will be concatenated and appear in the result.

Let the attribute names of R be $R_1, \ldots R_m$ and the attribute names of S be $S_1, \ldots S_n$ with no common attribute names between R and S. Then the attribute values $r_1, \ldots r_m, s_1, \ldots s_n$ form a row in the result relation with each r_i in the column for R_i and each s_i in the column for S_i if and only if:

1) $r_1, \ldots r_m$ form a row in R with each r_i in the column for R_i and $s_1, \ldots s_n$ form a row in S with each s_i in the column for S_i. That is, $r_1, \ldots r_m, s_1, \ldots s_n$ form a row in R TIMES S.

AND 2) $C_{R,S}$ evaluates to TRUE for the attribute values in $\{r_1, \ldots r_m\}$ and $\{s_1, \ldots s_n\}$.

Given any two relations R and S with no common attribute names and a comparison expression $C_{R,S}$ then the θ-Join of relations R and S subject to comparison $C_{R,S}$ is represented by the following expression:

R θ-Join($C_{R,S}$) S

θ-Join is not a primitive operation; it can be implemented by:
1) Taking the PRODUCT of the two input relations.
2) Using SELECT on the relation from 1) to select the rows that satisfy the comparison condition $C_{R,S}$.

θ-Join Properties: θ-Join is commutative and also distributive over UNION. We'll limit the consideration of associativity to a specific case, namely: Expressions of the form R θ-Join($C_{R,S}$) (S θ-Join($D_{S,T}$) T) and (R θ-Join($C_{R,S}$) S) θ-Join($D_{S,T}$) T are associative.

Thus let R, S, and T be relations with no common attribute names. Further, let $C_{R,S}$ be a comparison condition between R and S; let $D_{S,T}$ be a comparison between S and T. Then we have:

Commutivity: R θ-Join($C_{R,S}$) S = S θ-Join($C_{R,S}$) R.

Associativity: R θ-Join($C_{R,S}$) (S θ-Join($D_{S,T}$) T) = (R θ-Join($C_{R,S}$) S) θ-Join($D_{S,T}$) T.

If R and S are relations with no common attribute names; S and T are UNION compatible, then:

Distributivity over UNION: R θ-Join($C_{R,S}$) (S UNION T) = (R θ-Join($C_{R,S}$) S) UNION (R θ-Join($C_{R,S}$) T).

Note that $C_{R,S}$ is defined for R and T because T and S are union compatible and thus have the same attributes.

Example: θ-Join (Theta-Join)

Each row of the Instructors relation on the right contains an instructor name, subject and level (1 to 4) that the instructor is qualified to teach. An instructor can also teach that subject at all lower levels.

Instructors

Name	Subject	Level
Wilson	English	3
Lenox	Math	4
Jones	Business	2
Peterson	Science	3
Barret	English	4
Lenox	Science	4

The PlannedCourses relation on the right lists the courses and level that will be offered next semester. For simplicity, we've prefixed the subject and level by "P" to allow us to do a θ-Join with the Instructors relation. Otherwise, we would've had to rename these attributes to be different from the corresponding attributes in Instructors.

PlannedCourses

PSubject	PLevel
English	2
Math	3
Business	2
Science	4
English	4

Define a comparison expression, $C_{Instructors, PlannedCourses}$, as "Subject = PSubject AND Level ≥ PLevel."

Performing the Theta-Join operation on Instructors and Planned Courses subject to the comparison expression yields the relation to the right.

Instructors θ-Join($C_{Instructors, PlannedCourses}$) PlannedCourses

Name	Subject	Level	PSubject	PLevel
Wilson	English	3	English	2
Barret	English	4	English	2
Lenox	Math	4	Math	3
Jones	Business	2	Business	2
Lenox	Science	4	Science	4
Barret	English	4	English	4

Finally, we take the projection of the preceding relation on the set of attributes {Name, PSubject, PLevel}. This gives the possible instructors for each of the planned courses.

Possible Instructors

Name	PSubject	PLevel
Wilson	English	2
Barret	English	2
Lenox	Math	3
Jones	Business	2
Lenox	Science	4
Barret	English	4

Equi-Join: A special case of the θ-Join where the comparison is always "=" and the comparison expression is constructed from these comparisons with the AND operator. Thus, for relations R and S with no attributes names in common, the comparison expression has the following form:

$(X_1 = Y_1)$ AND $(X_2 = Y_2)$ …AND $(X_K = Y_K)$ where X_i, Y_i are attribute names from R and S respectively.

Equi-Join Properties: The properties are the same as for the θ-Join. Namely, Equi-Join is commutative and also distributive over UNION. Expressions of the form R Equi-Join($C_{R,S}$) (S Equi-Join($D_{S,T}$) T) and (R Equi-Join($C_{R,S}$) S) Equi-Join($D_{S,T}$) T are associative.

Thus let R, S and T be relations with no common attribute names. Then we have:

Commutivity: R Equi-Join($C_{R,S}$) S = S Equi-Join($C_{R,S}$) R.
Associativity: R Equi-Join($C_{R,S}$) (S Equi-Join($D_{S,T}$) T) = (R Equi-Join($C_{R,S}$) S) Equi-Join($D_{S,T}$) T.

If R and S have no common attributes and S and T are UNION compatible, then the following holds:

Distributivity over UNION: R Equi-Join($C_{R,S}$) (S UNION T) = (R Equi-Join($C_{R,S}$) S) UNION (R Equi-Join($C_{R,S}$) T). (Note that since T and S are union compatible and thus have the same attributes, $C_{R,S}$ can be evaluated for R and T.)

The "Natural Join" will be concerned with relations that have common attributes. We'll present the usual "binary" definition for two relations and also a "general" definition that pertains to any number of relations.

Natural Join (Join): Given two relations, construct a new relation by concatenating those pairs of rows – one from each relation – for which each common attribute value in the row from the first relation equals the corresponding common attribute value in the row from the second. Note that in contrast to the θ-Join (and therefore the Equi-Join) the two relations may have common attribute names. One could use the re-name operation to ensure that corresponding attributes have the same name. The heading will be comprised of all the attribute names in both input relations except that duplicate attribute names are eliminated. The Natural Join is usually referred to simply as the "Join."

Binary Definition of Join: Let R be a relation with attribute names R_1, …R_m, C_1, …C_k and S a relation with attribute names S_1, …S_n, C_1, …C_k. The common attributes of R and S are C_1, …C_k and the heading of the result relation of the natural join of R and S is R_1, …R_m, S_1, …S_n, C_1, …C_k. Then, the attribute values r_1, …r_m, s_1, …s_n, c_1, …c_k form a row in the result relation with each r_i in the column for R_i, s_i in the column for S_i and c_i in the column for C_i if and only if:

1) r_1, …r_m, c_1, …c_k form a row in R with each r_i in the column for R_i and c_i in the column for C_i.
AND 2) s_1, …s_n, c_1, …c_k form a row, in S with each s_i in the column for S_i and c_i in the column for C_i.

Natural join is not a primitive operation; it can be defined as follows:
1) RENAME any common attributes in one of the relations.
2) Take the PRODUCT of the relations from 2).
3) Get a comparison condition that uses the renamed attributes and ensures the equality of the original common attributes. That is, let C_1, …C_m be the common attributes between R and S and let these attributes in S be renamed to $S.C_1$, …$S.C_m$. Then the comparison condition would be $C_1 = S.C_1$, …$C_m = S.C_m$.
4) SELECT those rows from 2) that satisfy the comparison condition from 3).
5) PROJECT on all the columns except the renamed attributes $S.C_1$, …$S.C_m$.

Natural Join Properties: Join is commutative, associative and distributive over UNION. Thus we have:
Commutivity: R Join S = S Join R.
Associativity: R Join (S Join T) = (R Join S) Join T.

Let T be UNION compatible with S. Then the following holds:
Distributivity over UNION: R Join (S UNION T) = (R JOIN S) UNION (R JOIN T).

Inference 3.3.1: The natural join of two relations with no common attributes is equivalent to their product.

Example 1: Equi-Join

The relation Emp/Proj below left contains project IDs and the employee(s) assigned to work on them. The relation Projects below right lists the project name for each project ID. The attribute name ProjID has been renamed to Project.ProjID to avoid common attribute names between these relations and thereby enable us to do an Equi-Join with the comparison expression "ProjID = Project.ProjID."

Emp/Proj

EmpID	ProjID
E14	P12
E14	P76
E01	P76
E18	P12
E18	P20
E18	P16

Projects

Project.ProjID	ProjName
P12	Prepare Bid for Wilson Account
P76	Replace Desktops in Engr. Dep.
P20	Complete Five Year Plan
P16	Develop Pricing for Product A

The result of doing the Equi-Join appears below. Each row of this result relation contains an Employee ID of an employee assigned to a project along with the name of the project. As expected for Equi-Join, the extraneous column Projects.ProjID appears.

Emp/Proj Equi-Join("ProjID=Project.ProjID") Projects

EmpID	ProjID	Project.ProjID	ProjName
E14	P12	P12	Prepare Bid for Wilson Account
E14	P76	P76	Replace Desktops in Engr. Dep.
E01	P76	P76	Replace Desktops in Engr. Dep.
E18	P12	P12	Prepare Bid for Wilson Account
E18	P20	P20	Complete Five Year Plan
E18	P16	P16	Develop Pricing for Product A

Example 2: Join (Natural Join)

The same input relations as in Example 1 are presented below except that there is no need to rename the ProjID attribute in Projects because we'll be doing a Join rather than an Equi-Join.

Emp/Proj

EmpID	ProjID
E14	P12
E14	P76
E01	P76
E18	P12
E18	P20
E18	P16

Projects

ProjID	ProjName
P12	Prepare Bid for Wilson Account
P76	Replace Desktops in Engr. Dep.
P20	Complete Five Year Plan
P16	Develop Pricing for Product A

The result of Emp/Proj Join Projects appears below. There is no extra column listing the project IDs because Join eliminates duplicate columns.

Emp/Proj Join Projects

EmpID	ProjID	ProjName
E14	P12	Prepare Bid for Wilson Account
E14	P76	Replace Desktops in Engr. Dep.
E01	P76	Replace Desktops in Engr. Dep.
E18	P12	Prepare Bid for Wilson Account
E18	P20	Complete Five Year Plan
E18	P16	Develop Pricing for Product A

The foregoing "binary" definition of join is useful for constructing a join of two relations and emphasizes that rows with equal common values are concatenated. The equivalent "general" definition below from reference [ABU] is valuable for analyzing the join of any number of relations.

General Definition of Join: Let $R_1, R_2, \ldots R_n$ be a collection of relations. Then the result of the Natural Join of these relations has a heading with all the attribute names $A_1, A_2, \ldots A_m$ such that every A_i appears in at least one of $R_1, R_2, \ldots R_n$ and consists of all the rows $(a_1, a_2, \ldots a_m)$ where:

The values in $\{a_1, a_2, \ldots a_m\}$ corresponding to the attributes of R_i form a row in R_i for all $1 \leq i \leq n$.

Inference 3.3.2: The General Definition of Join is equivalent to the Binary Definition.

The following expression represents the natural join of any two relations R and S.

R JOIN S

Outer Joins: There is a Left Outer Join, Right Outer Join and Full Outer Join corresponding to each of the three types of Inner Joins. Hence, there is a Left Outer θ-Join, Left Outer Equi-Join, Left Outer Natural Join – also called simply the Left Outer Join – and similar Right and Full Outer Joins.

Left Outer θ-Join: Given two relations with no common attribute names and a comparison expression of the form used for an inner θ-Join, construct a new relation containing all the rows from the corresponding θ-Join of the relations plus all the rows of the left relation that did not appear in the Inner Join filled out with nulls for the values of the right relation. As with the θ-Join, the heading will be comprised of all the attribute names of both input relations.

Let the attribute names of a relation R be $R_1, \ldots R_m$ and the attribute names of S be $S_1, \ldots S_n$ with no common attributes between R and S. Let $C_{R,S}$ be a comparison expression on some attributes of R and S. Then the attribute values $r_1, \ldots r_m, s_1, \ldots s_n$ form a row in the result relation with each r_i in the column for R_i and each s_i in the column for S_i if and only if:

Either 1) $r_1, \ldots r_m, s_1, \ldots s_n$ form a row in (R θ-Join($C_{R,S}$) S) with each r_i in the column for R_i and each s_i in the column for S_i.
Or 2) The values $r_1, \ldots r_m$ form a row in R with each r_i in the column for R_i, but do not appear together in any row of the corresponding θ-Join and $s_1, \ldots s_n$ are all null.

We'll use the following to represent the Left Outer θ-Join of relations R and S subject to comparison $C_{R,S}$:

R LEFT OUTER θ-JOIN($C_{R,S}$) S

Left Outer θ-Join is not a primitive operation. For any two relations – R with attributes $R_1, \ldots R_n$ and S with attributes $S_1, \ldots S_m$ – with no attributes in common and comparison expression $C_{R,S}$, it can be implemented from primitive operations as follows (which is based on the procedure found in [Da2]):

1) Let A = R MINUS (PROJECT ((R θ-Join($C_{R,S}$) S), $\{R_1, \ldots R_n\}$). The rows in A are the rows in R that don't appear in R θ-Join $C_{R,S}$) S. That is, they don't match any rows in S for condition $C_{R,S}$.
2) Let SNull be the relation with the same heading as S consisting of one row with all null values.
3) Let B = A TIMES SNull. Then B is comprised of the set of all rows from R that are not in R θ-Join ($C_{R,S}$) S filled out with nulls for the values of the attributes from S.
4) Then, R LEFT OUTER θ-Join($C_{R,S}$) S = (R θ-Join($C_{R,S}$) S) UNION B. Recall that θ-Join($C_{R,S}$) is definable using PRODUCT and SELECT. It follows that Left Outer θ-Join($C_{R,S}$) is definable.

Left Outer θ-Join Properties: Left Outer θ-Join is not commutative or distributive over UNION. Expressions of the form R Left Outer θ-Join($C_{R,S}$) (S Left Outer θ-Join($D_{S,T}$) T) and (R Left Outer θ-Join($C_{R,S}$) S) Left Outer θ-Join($D_{S,T}$) T are associative. Thus let R, S, and T be relations with no common attribute names where $C_{R,S}$ is a comparison condition between R and S; let $D_{S,T}$ be a comparison between S and T. Then the following holds:

Associativity: R Left Outer θ-Join($C_{R,S}$)(S Left Outer θ-Join($D_{S,T}$) T) = (R Left Outer θ-Join($C_{R,S}$) S) Left Outer θ-Join($D_{S,T}$) T.

Example: Left Outer θ-Join

Each row of the Instructors relation below left contains an instructor name, subject and level (1 to 4) that the instructor is qualified to teach. An instructor can also teach that subject at all lower levels.

The PlannedCourses relation below right lists the courses and level that will be offered next semester. For simplicity, we've prefixed the subject and level by P to allow us to do a Left Outer θ-Join with the Instructors relation. Otherwise, we would've had to rename these attributes to be different from the corresponding attributes in Instructors.

<table>
<tr><th colspan="3" align="center">Instructors</th></tr>
<tr><th>Name</th><th>Subject</th><th>Level</th></tr>
<tr><td>Wilson</td><td>English</td><td>3</td></tr>
<tr><td>Lenox</td><td>Math</td><td>4</td></tr>
<tr><td>Lenox</td><td>Science</td><td>4</td></tr>
<tr><td>Jones</td><td>Business</td><td>2</td></tr>
<tr><td>Peterson</td><td>Science</td><td>3</td></tr>
<tr><td>Peterson</td><td>Math</td><td>2</td></tr>
<tr><td>Barret</td><td>English</td><td>4</td></tr>
<tr><td>Henson</td><td>History</td><td>3</td></tr>
<tr><td>Carter</td><td>French</td><td>1</td></tr>
</table>

PlannedCourses	
PSubject	PLevel
English	2
English	4
Math	3
Business	2
Business	3
Science	4
French	2
French	1

Let a comparison expression $C_{\text{Instructors, PlannedCourses}}$ be "Subject = PSubject AND Level ≥ PLevel"

Performing the indicated Left Outer θ-Join results in the relation below. This gives the possible instructors for each of the planned courses and shows – by Nulls in the PSubject and PLevel columns – what combinations of (instructor name, subject, level) are not of use for the planned courses.

Instructors Left Outer θ-Join("Subject = PSubject AND Level ≥ PLevel") PlannedCourses

Name	Subject	Level	PSubject	PLevel
Wilson	English	3	English	2
Lenox	Math	4	Math	3
Lenox	Science	4	Science	4
Jones	Business	2	Business	2
Peterson	Science	3	Null	Null
Peterson	Math	2	Null	Null
Barret	English	4	English	2
Barret	English	4	English	4
Henson	History	3	Null	Null
Carter	French	1	French	1

Note that the nulls used to fill out a row in a Left Outer θ-Join – and in the left outer joins to follow – don't mean that the values are unknown or not applicable. Rather, they indicate that the values for the left relation on that row don't match any row in the right relation.

Left Outer Equi-Join: The Left Outer Equi-Join is a special case of the Left Outer θ-Join where the corresponding inner join is the Equi-Join. We'll represent it by the expression:

R LEFT OUTER EQUI-JOIN($C_{R,S}$) S

<u>Left Outer Equi-Join Properties</u>: Left Outer Equi -Join is not commutative or distributive over UNION. Expressions of the form R Left Outer Equi-Join($C_{R,S}$) (S Left Outer Equi-Join($D_{S,T}$) T) and (R Left Outer Equi-Join($C_{R,S}$) S) Left Outer Equi-Join($D_{S,T}$) T are associative. Thus let R, S, and T be relations with no common attribute names where $C_{R,S}$ is a comparison condition between R and S; let $D_{S,T}$ be a comparison between S and T. Then the following holds:

Associativity: R Left Outer Equi-Join($C_{R,S}$) (S Left Outer Equi-Join($D_{S,T}$) T) = (R Left Outer Equi-Join($C_{R,S}$) S) Left Outer Equi-Join($D_{S,T}$) T.

Left Outer Natural Join: Given any two relations, construct a new relation with the heading comprised of all the attribute names of both input relations except that duplicate attribute names are eliminated. It will contain all the rows from the corresponding Natural Join plus all the rows of the left relation that did not appear in the inner join filled out with nulls for the non-common attribute values of the right relation.

Let R be a relation with attribute names $R_1, \ldots R_m, C_1, \ldots C_k$ and S a relation with attribute names $S_1, \ldots S_n, C_1, \ldots C_k$. The common attributes of R and S are $C_1, \ldots C_k$ and the heading of the result relation of the left outer natural join of R and S is $R_1, \ldots R_m, S_1, \ldots S_n, C_1, \ldots C_k$. Then, the attribute values $r_1, \ldots r_m, s_1, \ldots s_n, c_1, \ldots c_k$ form a row in the result relation with each r_i in the column for R_i, s_i in the column for S_i and c_i in the column for C_i if and only if:

Either 1) $r_1, \ldots r_m, c_1, \ldots c_k, s_1, \ldots s_n$ form a row in (R Join S) with each r_i in the column for R_i, each c_i in the column for C_i and each s_i in the column for S_i.
Or 2) The values $r_1, \ldots r_m, c_1, \ldots c_k$ form a row in R but don't appear together in any row of the corresponding Join and $s_1, \ldots s_n$ are all null.

Inference 3.3.3: The left outer join of two relations with no common attributes equals their product.

The following expression represents the left outer natural join of any two relations R and S.

R LEFT OUTER JOIN S

Left Outer Natural Join is not a primitive operation. For any two relations – R with attributes $R_1, \ldots R_m, C_1, \ldots C_k$ and S with attributes $S_1, \ldots S_n, C_1, \ldots C_k$ – it can be implemented from basic operations as follows (which is similar to the procedure given previously for Left Outer θ-Join):

1) Let A = R MINUS (PROJECT ((R JOIN S), $\{R_1, \ldots R_m, C_1, \ldots C_k\}$). The rows in A are the rows in R that don't appear in R JOIN S. That is, they don't match any rows in S.
2) Let SNull be the relation with heading $S_1, \ldots S_n$ having just one row of all null values.
3) Let B = A TIMES SNull. Then B is comprised of the set of all the rows from R that are not in R JOIN S filled out with nulls for the values of the S attributes $S_1, \ldots S_n$.
4) Then, R LEFT OUTER JOIN S = (R JOIN S) UNION B. Recall that JOIN is definable using RENAME, PRODUCT, SELECT and PROJECT. It follows that LEFT OUTER JOIN is definable.

<u>Left Outer Natural-Join Properties</u>: Left Outer Join is not commutative and not distributive over UNION. It's also not generally associative; however, the following restriction is sufficient to ensure associativity: The adjoining relations must have at least one attribute in common, but the relations on the far left and far right of the expression have no attributes in common. That is, we have the following.

Associativity with Restriction: Let R, S and T be relations where R and S have at least one attribute in common; S and T have at least one attribute in common; R and T have no attributes in common. Then:

R Left Outer Join (S Left Outer Join T) = (R Left Outer Join S) Left Outer Join T.

Example 1: Left Outer Join

For each Project ID, the Proj relation below left gives the Project Name.

Each row of the Emp/Proj relation below right contains a Project ID and the ID of an employee assigned to work on that project. An employee can be assigned to more than one project.

Proj	
ProjID	ProjName
P12	Prepare Bid for Wilson Account
P76	Replace Desktops in Engr. Dept.
P20	Complete Five Year Plan
P16	Develop Pricing for Product A

Emp/Proj	
EmpID	ProjID
E14	P12
E14	P76
E01	P76
E18	P12
E18	P20

The result of Proj LEFT OUTER JOIN Emp/Proj appears below. For any row in this result relation, the employee with EmpID is assigned to the project with ProjID and name ProjName. A Null in the EmpID column indicates that no one has been assigned to this project.

Proj LEFT OUTER JOIN Emp/Proj

ProjID	ProjName	EmpID
P12	Prepare Bid for Wilson Account	E14
P12	Prepare Bid for Wilson Account	E18
P76	Replace Desktops in Engr. Dep.	E14
P76	Replace Desktops in Engr. Dep.	E01
P20	Complete Five Year Plan	E18
P16	Develop Pricing for Product A	Null

Example 2: Non Associativity of Left Outer Join

This will be demonstrated by three examples. Let Relations R, S and T have values as below where Left Outer Join is denoted by LOJ. Note that none of the examples satisfy the restriction that ensures associativity; that is, "Adjoining relations must have at least one attribute in common and the relations on the far right and far left have no attributes in common."

R	S	T	R LOJ (S LOJ T)			(R LOJ S) LOJ T		
A	B	A | C	A	B	C	A	B	C
1	1	2 | 1	1	Null	Null	1	1	Null

R	S	T	R LOJ (S LOJ T)		(R LOJ S) LOJ T	
A	A	B	A	B	A	B
1	2	1	1	Null	1	1

R		S		T		R LOJ (S LOJ T)			(R LOJ S) LOJ T		
A	B	A	C	B	C	A	B	C	A	B	C
1	1	1	2	1	1	1	1	Null	1	1	2

– Section 3.3: Left Outer Natural Join –

Right Outer Joins: Right outer joins are identical to left outer joins except that the roles of the right and left relations are reversed: We include all the rows of the related inner join plus the rows from the right relation that did not appear in the inner join with nulls for the left relation columns. In the case of the Right Outer Natural Join, only the non-common attributes are filled out with Nulls.

The following inference states that right outer joins are equivalent to the corresponding left outer joins with the positions of the left and right input relations reversed.

Inference 3.3.4:
R Right Outer θ-Join($C_{R,S}$) S = S Left Outer θ-Join($C_{R,S}$) R.
R Right Outer Equi-Join($C_{R,S}$) S = S Left Outer Equi-Join($C_{R,S}$) R.
R Right Outer Join S = S Left Outer Join R.

The right outer joins are all non-primitive with the same properties as for the corresponding left outer joins.

Properties of Right Outer Joins: The right outer joins are all non-commutative and not distributive over UNION. Expressions of the form R Right Outer θ-Join($C_{R,S}$) (S Right Outer θ-Join($D_{S,T}$) T) and (R Right Outer θ-Join($C_{R,S}$) S) Right Outer θ-Join($D_{S,T}$) T and the corresponding expressions for Right Outer Equi-Join are associative. Right Outer Join is associative when the adjoining relations have at least one attribute in common, but the relations on the far left and the far right of the expression have no attributes in common. Thus we have the following statements of associativity for right outer joins:

R Right Outer θ-Join($C_{R,S}$)(S Right Outer θ-Join($D_{S,T}$) T) = (R Right Outer θ-Join($C_{R,S}$) S) Right Outer θ-Join($D_{S,T}$) T.
R Right Outer Equi-Join($C_{R,S}$) (S Right Outer Equi-Join($D_{S,T}$) T) = (R Right Outer Equi-Join($C_{R,S}$) S) Right Outer Equi-Join($D_{S,T}$) T.

Let R, S and T be relations where R and S have at least one attribute in common; S and T have at least one attribute in common; R and T have no attributes in common. Then:
R Right Outer Join (S Right Outer Join T) = (R Right Outer Join S) Right Outer Join T.

Full Outer Joins: The full outer joins combine the action of the left and right outer joins. Again, there is a full outer join corresponding to the θ-Join, Equi-Join and Natural Join. The heading is the same as for the corresponding inner join. It contains the rows from the inner join and also all the rows from the left and right relations that were not in the inner join filled out with nulls for the attribute values of the other relation. In the case of the Full Outer Natural Join, only the non-common attributes are filled out with Nulls.

Inference 3.3.5: The full outer join of two relations is equal to the UNION of the corresponding left and right outer joins. Thus:
R Full Outer θ-Join($C_{R,S}$) S = (R Left Outer θ-Join($C_{R,S}$) S) UNION (R Right Outer θ-Join($C_{R,S}$) S).
R Full Outer Equi-Join($C_{R,S}$) S=(R Left Outer Equi-Join($C_{R,S}$) S)UNION(R Right Outer Equi-Join($C_{R,S}$) S).
R Full Outer Join S = (R Left Outer Join S) UNION (R Right Outer Join S).

The full outer joins are all non-primitive.

Properties of the Full Outer Joins: The full outer joins are all commutative but not distributive over UNION. They're associative subject to the following restrictions:

As for θ-Join, expressions of the form R Full Outer θ-Join($C_{R,S}$) (S Full Outer θ-Join($D_{S,T}$) T) and (R Full θ-Join($C_{R,S}$) S) Full θ-Join($D_{S,T}$) T and the corresponding Full Outer Equi-Join expressions are associative.

Full Outer Join is associative with the restriction that the adjoining relations have at least one attribute in common and the relations on the far left and the far right of the expression have no attributes in common.

Example: Full Outer θ-Join

Each row of the Instructors relation below left contains an instructor name, subject and level (1 to 4) that the instructor is qualified to teach. An instructor can also teach that subject at all lower levels.

The PlannedCourses relation below right lists the courses and level that will be offered next semester. For simplicity, we've prefixed the subject and level by P to allow us to do a θ-Join with the Instructors relation. Otherwise, we would've had to rename these attributes to be different from the corresponding attributes in Instructors.

Instructors

Name	Subject	Level
Wilson	English	3
Lenox	Math	4
Lenox	Science	4
Jones	Business	2
Peterson	Science	3
Peterson	Math	2
Barret	English	4
Henson	History	3
Carter	French	1

PlannedCourses

PSubject	PLevel
English	2
English	4
Math	3
Business	2
Business	3
Science	4
French	2
French	1

Let a comparison expression $C_{Instructors, PlannedCourses}$ be "Subject = PSubject AND Level ≥ PLevel"

Performing the indicated Full Outer θ-Join results in the relation below. This gives the possible instructors for each of the planned courses and shows – by Nulls in the PSubject and PLevel columns – what combinations of (instructor name, subject, level) are not of use for the planned courses. It also reveals – by Nulls in the Name, Subject and Level columns – the planned courses for which there are no suitable instructors.

Instructors Full Outer θ-Join("Subject = PSubject AND Level ≥ PLevel") PlannedCourses

Name	Subject	Level	PSubject	PLevel
Wilson	English	3	English	2
Lenox	Math	4	Math	3
Lenox	Science	4	Science	4
Jones	Business	2	Business	2
Peterson	Science	3	Null	Null
Peterson	Math	2	Null	Null
Barret	English	4	English	2
Barret	English	4	English	4
Henson	History	3	Null	Null
Carter	French	1	French	1
Null	Null	Null	French	2
Null	Null	Null	Business	3

Let $C_{R,S}$ and $D_{S,T}$ be comparison expressions on the indicated relations. We then have:

Commutivity:
R Full Outer θ-Join($C_{R,S}$) S = S Full Outer θ-Join($C_{R,S}$) R.
R Full Outer Equi-Join($C_{R,S}$) S = S Full Outer Equi-Join($C_{R,S}$) R.
R Full Outer Join($C_{R,S}$) S = S Full Outer Join($C_{R,S}$) R.

Associativity:
R Full Outer θ-Join($C_{R,S}$) (S Full Outer θ-Join($D_{S,T}$) T)=(R Full Outer θ-Join($C_{R,S}$)S) Full θ-Join($D_{S,T}$) T.
R Full Outer Equi-Join($C_{R,S}$) (S Full Outer Equi-Join($D_{S,T}$)T)=(R Full Outer Equi-Join($C_{R,S}$)S) Full Outer Equi-Join($D_{S,T}$) T.

Let R, S and T be relations where R and S have at least one attribute in common; S and T have at least one attribute in common; R and T have no attributes in common. Then:
R Full Outer Join (S Full Outer Join T) = (R Full Outer Join S) Full Outer Join T.

Implementing Joins in SQL: Use the From and On clauses of the SQL select statement.

Like the various joins, the "Divide" operator is an offshoot of the product operator. Though not as intuitive as the other operators, it's useful for finding those attribute values in a relation that each occur with all specified values of some other attributes in the relation.

For the following, recall that a "proper" subset is one that doesn't contain all the items in the original set.

Divide: Given a relation R and a relation S – whose attributes are a proper subset of the attributes of R – construct a new relation with a heading of all the attributes in R that are not in S. The rows will be all the values that form a row in R when concatenated with any row in S.

Let R be a relation with attributes $R_1, \ldots R_m, S_1, \ldots S_n$ and let S be a relation with attributes $S_1, \ldots S_n$. Then $r_1, r_2 \ldots r_m$ is a row in "R divided by S" with each r_i in the column for R_i if and only if:

1) $r_1, r_2 \ldots r_m$ is a row in PROJECT(R, $\{R_1, \ldots R_m\}$) with each r_i in the column for R_i.

AND 2) $r_1, r_2 \ldots r_m, s_1, s_2 \ldots s_n$ is a row in R with each r_i in the column for R_i and s_i in the column for S_i for any set of values $s_1, s_2 \ldots s_n$ that is a row in S.

For relations R and S where the attributes of S are a proper subset of the attributes of R, we'll use the following expression to denote R divided by S:

R DIVIDEDBY S

Divide is not a primitive operation; one can construct it from other operations as follows:
1) Let A= PROJECT(R, $\{R_1, \ldots R_m\}$) TIMES S. A will consist of the rows $r_1, r_2 \ldots r_m, s_1, s_2 \ldots s_n$ where $r_1, r_2 \ldots r_m$ is a row in PROJECT(R, $\{R_1, \ldots R_m\}$) and $s_1, s_2 \ldots s_n$ is a row in S.
2) Let B = A MINUS R. B will consist of the rows $r_1, r_2 \ldots r_m, s_1, s_2 \ldots s_n$ that are not in R where $s_1, s_2 \ldots s_n$ is a row in S.
3) Let C = PROJECT(B, $\{R_1, \ldots R_m\}$). C consists of the rows $r_1, r_2 \ldots r_m$ for which there exists values $s_1, s_2 \ldots s_n$ that form a row in S where $r_1, r_2 \ldots r_m, s_1, s_2 \ldots s_n$ isn't a row in R.
4) Let D = PROJECT(R, $\{R_1, \ldots R_m\}$) MINUS C. Then D will contain rows $r_1, r_2 \ldots r_m$ such that if $s_1, s_2 \ldots s_n$ is a row in S, then $r_1, r_2 \ldots r_m, s_1, s_2 \ldots s_n$ is a row in R. Thus R DIVEDEDBY S = D.

Divide Properties: Divide is not commutative and not associative. It is distributive over UNION.

Let R, S, and T be relations such that the attributes of S are a proper subset of the attributes of R. Also, assume that S and T are union compatible. Then we have:

R DIVIDEDBY (S UNION T) = (R DIVIDEDBY S) UNION (R DIVIDEDBY T)

Implementing Divide in SQL: Since Divide is not primitive, it can be constructed from the SQL implementations of PROJECT, TIMES, and MINUS.

Example: Divide Operator

Each row of the "Instructors" relation on the right contains an instructor name, subject and level (1 to 4) that the instructor is qualified to teach. An instructor can also teach that subject at all lower levels.

Suppose we wish to find the instructors who are qualified to teach all levels of both math and science.

Instructors

Name	Subject	Level
Wilson	English	3
Lenox	Math	4
Jones	Business	2
Peterson	Science	4
Barret	English	4
Lenox	Science	4
Henson	History	3
Carter	French	1
Peterson	Math	4

The "Courses" relation on the right lists the subjects and levels for which we would like to find all qualified instructors.

Courses

Subject	Level
Math	4
Science	4

The relation resulting from the operation "Instructors DIVIDEDBY Courses" appears to the right. This is the desired list of instructors qualified to teach all levels of both math and science. We demonstrate how this relation could be constructed below.

Name
Lenox
Peterson

The following steps can obtain the result relation of "Instructors DIVIDEDBY Courses":

1) A = PROJECT(Instructors, Name) TIMES Courses. This will contain all the values of Name from "Instructors" combined with the row values of Courses.

On the right, we show six rows for relation A.

Name	Subject	Level
Wilson	Math	4
Wilson	Science	4
Lenox	Math	4
Lenox	Science	4
Jones	Math	4
Jones	Science	4
Etc.....		

2) B = A Minus Instructors. This has the rows that are not in Instructors but {Subject, Level} is in Courses.

On the right, we show four rows for relation B. The rows for Lenox in relation A do not appear in B because they appear in Instructors and were therefore removed by the Minus operator.

Name	Subject	Level
Wilson	Math	4
Wilson	Science	4
Jones	Math	4
Jones	Science	4
Etc.....		

3) C= Project(B, Name). This consists of the values of Name for which there is a value of {Subject, Level} in Courses where {Name, Subject, Level} is not a row in Instructors.

On the right, we show four rows for relation C.

Name
Wilson
Wilson
Jones
Jones
Etc....

4) D = Project(Instructors, Name) Minus C contains the rows which form a row in Instructors when combined with any row in Courses.

That is, we have Instructors DIVIDEDBY Courses.

Name
Lenox
Petersen

We conclude this chapter with a summary of the operations covered, their properties and whether they are primitive.

Summary of Operator Properties

Operator	Commutative	Associative	Distributive Over UNION	Primitive	Operator
Rename	NA	NA	NA	Yes	Rename
Select	NA	NA	NA	Yes	Select
Project	NA	NA	NA	Yes	Project
Union	Yes	Yes	NA	Yes	Union
Difference	No	No	No[1]	Yes	Difference
Intersect	Yes	Yes	Yes	No	Intersect
Product	Yes	Yes	Yes	Yes	Product
θ-Join	Yes	Yes[2]	Yes	No	θ-Join
Equi-Join	Yes	Yes[2]	Yes	No	Equi-Join
Join	Yes	Yes	Yes	No	Join
Left Outer θ-Join	No	Yes[2]	No	No	Left Outer θ-Join
Left Outer Equi-Join	No	Yes[2]	No	No	Left Outer Equi-Join
Left Outer Join	No	Yes[3]	No	No	Left Outer Join
Right Outer θ-Join	No	Yes[2]	No	No	Right Outer θ-Join
Right Outer Equi-Join	No	Yes[2]	No	No	Right Outer Equi-Join
Right Outer Join	No	Yes[3]	No	No	Right Outer Join
Full Outer θ-Join	Yes	Yes[2]	No	No	Full Outer θ-Join
Full Outer Equi-Join	Yes	Yes[2]	No	No	Full Outer Equi-Join
Full Outer Join	Yes	Yes[3]	No	No	Full Outer Join
Divide	No	No	Yes	No	Divide

[1] Minus is not distributive over UNION in the usual left to right sense as R Minus (S UNION T). However, it is distributive over UNION "from the right" as (R UNION S) Minus T.

[2] Expressions of the form R θ-Join($C_{R,S}$) (S θ-Join($D_{S,T}$) T) and (R θ-Join($C_{R,S}$) S) θ-Join($D_{S,T}$) T are associative. This also holds if we replace θ-Join by Equi-Join and by the corresponding Outer Joins.

[3] Though not associative in general, the following restriction is sufficient to ensure associativity: The adjoining relations have at least one attribute in common and the relations on the far left and far right have no attributes in common.

Chapter 4
Dependence and Decomposition

In Chapter 1 we discussed how to use a type of table, called a relation, to model real world entities in a database. It's possible for a relation – though it may accurately model some entity – to have a correspondence or "dependency" between certain groups of its attributes that can be problematic. We'll look at the problems that this dependency causes when we discuss Normalization in Chapter 5.

In this Chapter we'll examine the types of dependencies that occur and also see that for each type there is a way to replace the relation with two or more relations that eliminate the dependence. In the next chapter, we'll see that this replacement process – called decomposition – is the basis for normalization.

Section 4.1 Functional Dependence

The possible values of some attributes in a relation may be restricted by the values of other attributes. The nature of this restriction is formalized and clarified by the definitions pertaining to Functional Dependence presented in this section.

Notation: Let $X = \{X_1, X_2 \ldots X_n\}$ be a set of attributes for some relation. Then an **X-Value** $= \{x_1, x_2 \ldots x_n\}$ is a set consisting of one value for each attribute in X.

Functional Dependence (FD): Let X and Y be sets of attributes for some relation, R. Then Y is functionally dependent on X if and only if whenever the X-values in two rows of R are equal, then the Y-values in those two rows are also equal.

Note that the terms "dependence" and "dependency" are used interchangeably.

A functional dependence is denoted by **X→Y**, which indicates that "Y is functionally dependent on X" or alternatively, "X functionally determines Y." (Note that "→" was also used to indicate a relation that references another in Section 2.2, however, the meaning should be clear by the context.)

Determinant and **Dependent**: Let X and Y be sets of attributes for some relation, R, such that X→Y. Then X is called the "determinant" of the functional dependence, X→Y, and Y is called the "dependent."

Inference 4.1.1: Let X and Y be sets of attributes for some relation, R, such that Y is a subset of X. Then it is always true that X→Y.

Trivial Functional Dependency: Let X and Y be sets of attributes for some relation, R, such that Y is a subset of X. Then the FD X→Y is called a "trivial functional dependency."

Inference 4.1.2: Let X, Y and Z be sets of attributes for some relation, R, such that X→Y and Y→Z. Then it is always true that X→Z.

Transitive Functional Dependency: Let X, Y and Z be sets of attributes for some relation, R, such that X→Y and Y→Z. Then the FD X→Z is called a "transitive functional dependency."

Left Irreducible Functional Dependency: Let X and Y be sets of attributes from some relation, R, such that X→Y. If Y is not functionally dependent on any subset of X, then X→Y is a called a "left irreducible functional dependency."

Full Functional Dependency: Means the same as "left irreducible functional dependency."

Terminology: If X→Y is a left irreducible functional dependency, then we say that Y is **Irreducibly Dependent** on X. Also, Y is said to be **Fully Dependent** on X.

Inference 4.1.3: Every set of attributes in a relation is functionally dependent on every super key (and thus also on every candidate key).

Inference 4.1.4: Let X and Y be sets of attributes for some relation. Then there is a non-trivial FD X→Y if and only if there is a non-trivial FD X→Y-X, where Y-X consists of all the attributes in Y but not in X.

Inference 4.1.5: Let X and $Y = \{Y_1, Y_2, \ldots Y_n\}$ be sets of attributes for some relation, where each Y_i is an attribute. Then X→Y if and only if $X \rightarrow Y_i$ for each i from 1 to n.

Inference 4.1.6: Let X and $Y = \{Y_1, Y_2, \ldots Y_n\}$ be sets of attributes for some relation, where each Y_i is an attribute. If there's a full FD $X \rightarrow Y_i$ for each i from 1 to n, then there's a full FD X→Y.

Example: Functional Dependence

Each row of the "Instructors" relation on the right contains the courses that each instructor has taught. Also included is the department that offers that course.

Instructors

Name	Course	Department
Wilson	Grammar I	English
Lenox	Algebra I	Math
Jones	Acct I	Business
Peterson	Algebra I	Math
Barret	Grammar I	English
Lenox	GenPhysics	Physics
Henson	AmHistory	History
Carter	French	Language

We can make the following observations about this relation:

1) {Course}→{Department}. The school has a rule that a course can be offered by only one department and, thus, there can never be two rows with the same value for Course and different values for Department. It follows, by definition, that the attribute Department is functionally dependent on Course.

2) Department isn't functionally dependent on Name because it's possible to have two rows where the value of Name is the same but the values of Department on those rows are different. For example, there are two rows where the value of Name is "Lenox" but the values of Department are different on those rows.

3) {Course}→{Department} is a full functional dependency because {Department} is not functionally dependent on any subset of {Course}.

4) {Name, Course}→{Department}. However, this is not a full functional dependency because Department is functionally dependent on {Course} that is a subset of {Name, Course}.

5) There is a non-trivial FD {Course}→{Course, Department}. However, to illustrate Inference 4.1.4, it's also true that {Course}→{Course, Department}-{Course}. That is, {Course}→{Department} is also non-trivial.

Armstrong's Axioms: Functional Dependencies can be shown to conform to rules known as "Armstrong's Axioms" that will be important when we discuss "Dependency Preservation." There are various equivalent lists of the axioms; the following is from reference [Da1], where W, X, Y, and Z are sets of attributes:

These rules follow from the definition of FD.	These follow from rules 1 – 3.
1. Reflexivity: If Y is a subset of X, then X→Y. (The above is the trivial FD.)	4. Self Determination: X→X.
	5. Decomposition: If X→YUZ, then X→Y and X→Z.
2. Augmentation: If X→Y, then XUZ→YUZ.	6. Union: If X→Y and X→Z, then X→YUZ.
3. Transitivity: If X→Y and Y→Z, then X→Z.	7. Composition: If X→Y and Z→W, then XUZ→YUW.

The following concept of a "minimal cover" will be used when we discuss "decomposition" in chapter 4.

Minimal Cover for a Set of Dependencies of a Relation: A set of functional dependencies, F, for some relation, R, is said to be a "Minimal Cover" for all the FDs in R if:

1. For every FD X→A in F, A contains just one attribute.
2. Every FD X→A in F is left irreducible.
3. All the FDs in R can be constructed from the FDs in F by using Armstrong's Axioms.
4. No FD can be eliminated from F without losing the ability to construct the FDs in R as in 3.

Example 1: Armstrong's Axioms

For relation "Orders", the order with "ONum" is for the customer with ID "CID" and name "CNam" located in sales region "CReg." We assume that CNam is unique for each customer.

Orders

ONum	CID	CNam	CReg
ON05	CN09	Wilco	R35
ON12	CN25	Martel	R28
ON34	CN09	Wilco	R35
ON26	CN18	Apex	R11
ON35	CN25	Martel	R28

1. Reflexivity: {ONum} is a subset of {ONum, CID}, thus {ONum, CID}→{ONum}.
2. Augmentation: {ONum}→{CID}, thus {ONum, CNam}→{CID, CNam}.
3. Transitivity: {ONum}→{CID} and {CID}→{CNam}, thus {ONum}→{CNam}.
4. Self Determination: {ONum}→{ONum}.
5. Decomposition: {ONum}→{CID, CNam}, thus {ONum}→{CID} and {ONum}→{CNam}.
6. Union: {ONum}→{CID} and {ONum}→{CNam}, thus {ONum}→{CID, CNam}.
7. Composition: {ONum}→{CID} and {CNam}→{CReg}, thus {ONum, CNam}→{CID, CReg}.

Example 2: Minimal Cover

Each row of the "Instructors" relation on the right contains the courses that each instructor has taught. Also included is the department that offers that course.

Instructors

Name	Course	Department
Wilson	Grammar I	English
Lenox	Algebra I	Math
Jones	Acct I	Business
Peterson	Algebra I	Math
Barret	Grammar I	English
Lenox	GenPhysics	Physics
Henson	AmHistory	History
Carter	French	Language

The non-trivial functional dependencies in relation "Instructors" are:

{Course}→{Department}, {Name, Course}→{Department} and {Course}→{Course, Department}.

We'll show that the set comprised of the FD {Course}→{Department} is a minimal cover for all the FDs in Instructor by verifying the 4 conditions in the definition.

1. The dependent of {Course}→{Department} contains just one attribute – Department.

2. {Course}→{Department} is left irreducible.

3. All the FDs in Instructors can be constructed from {Course}→{Department} by using Armstrong's Axioms as follows:

Using {Course}→{Department} and augmentation we have {Course ∪ Course}→{Course ∪ Department}. Thus {Course}→{Course, Department}.

Using reflexivity, {Name, Course}→Course. By transitivity with {Name, Course}→{Course} and {Course}→{Department} we have {Name, Course}→Department.

4. Finally, No FD can be eliminated from the set comprised of the FD {Course}→{Department} without losing the ability to construct the FDs in Instructors because there is only one FD in the set.

Since conditions 1-4 are met, the set consisting of the FD {Course}→{Department} is a minimal cover for all the FDs in Instructor.

Section 4.2 Multivalued Dependence

Multivalued Dependence is a generalization of Functional Dependence: instead of an X-value determining a single Y-value, an X-value can determine a set of Y-values.

In general, one must recognize and eliminate certain Multivalued Dependencies to attain one of the higher normal forms (fourth) that is discussed later. It's worth noting, however, that there are precautions one can take to minimize their occurrence as discussed in Note 5.1.1 in Section 5.1. Also, some common conditions are presented in Section 5.5 that may eliminate the need to check for multivalued dependencies.

Recall that for any set of attributes, X, an X-value is a set consisting of a value for each attribute in X.

Multivalued Dependency (MVD): Let R be a Relation whose attributes are partitioned into sets X, Y and Z such that each attribute of R is in exactly one of these sets. Then Y is multidependent on X if and only if for any two rows, r and s, with the same X-value, the set of Y-values from all rows with the same X and Z values as r is identical to the set of Y-values from all rows with the same X and Z values as s.

Notation: We denote a mulitivalued dependency by $X \rightarrow\rightarrow Y$, which indicates that "Y is multidependent on X" or equivalently, "X multidetermines Y."

The following inference amounts to an alternate and equivalent definition of multivalued dependencies.

Inference 4.2.1: Let R be a Relation and let the attributes of R be partitioned into X, Y and Z such that each attribute of R is in exactly one of these attribute sets. Then $X \rightarrow\rightarrow Y$ if and only if: any Y-value and Z-value that appear on rows with the same X-value also appear together on a row with that X-value. That is, if Y_1 appears on a row with X_1, and Z_1 appears on a row with X_1, then X_1, Y_1, and Z_1 appear on a row together.

MVDs occur in pairs: Since Y and Z are interchangeable in inference 4.2.1, it follows that $X \rightarrow\rightarrow Y$ if and only if $X \rightarrow\rightarrow Z$. Hence, we often write MVDs as $X \rightarrow\rightarrow Y \mid Z$.

Inference 4.2.2: Let R be a Relation and let the attributes of R be partitioned into subsets X and Y such that each attribute of R is in exactly one of these attribute sets. Then it is always true that $X \rightarrow\rightarrow Y$.

Trivial Multivalued Dependency: Let R be a Relation and let the attributes of R be partitioned into subsets X and Y such that each attribute of R is in exactly one of these attribute sets. Then the MVD $X \rightarrow\rightarrow Y$ is said to be a trivial multivalued dependency.

Inference 4.2.3: All FDs whose determinant and dependent have no attributes in common are also MVDs.

Inference 4.2.4: For any non-trivial FD $X \rightarrow Y$, the modified FD $X \rightarrow Y-X$ is an MVD. Note that if X and Y have no attributes in common, Y = Y-X.

Example: Multivalued Dependence

A manufacturer produces two types of refrigerators: one with the freezer on top and one with the freezer on the bottom. They offer the refrigerators with the top freezer in both white and almond; the bottom freezer models are offered only in white. The combinations of size and color for each type appear in the Refrigerators relation on the right.

Refrigerators

Freezer	Size	Color
Top	14.5	White
Top	18.5	White
Top	14.5	Almond
Top	18.5	Almond
Bottom	18.5	White
Bottom	22	White

We can make the following observations about this relation:

Freezer→→Size | Color. That is, Freezer multidetermines Size and Color. This follows because the set of all Color values corresponding to Freezer = Top, Size = 14.5 is {White, Almond}. This is the same as the set of all Color values for Freezer = Top, Size = 18.5. Also, the set of all Color values corresponding to Freezer = Bottom, Size = 18.5 is {White}. This is the same as the set of all Color values for Freezer = Bottom, Size = 22.

Suppose the manufacturer decided to offer the smaller bottom freezer model only in white and the larger bottom model only in almond. The new combinations of size and color for each type appear in the relation on the right where the value for Color has been changed from White to Almond on the last row.

Refrigerators

Freezer	Size	Color
Top	14.5	White
Top	18.5	White
Top	14.5	Almond
Top	18.5	Almond
Bottom	18.5	White
Bottom	22	***Almond***

For the modified Refrigerator relation, it's not true that Freezer multidetermines Size and Color. This is because the value of Color for Freezer = Bottom, Size = 18.5 is White. However, the value of Color for Freezer = Bottom, Size = 22 is Almond.

Section 4.3 Decomposition

This section defines decomposition and a particular type of decomposition called "Non-Loss." All of the higher normalization procedures (beyond the first) to be covered later depend on non-loss decomposition. We'll see that FDs and MVDs are the basis for ensuring that certain decompositions are non-loss and define a third type of dependency – Join Dependency – that's also closely linked to non-loss decomposition.

Decomposition: The process of replacing a relation by two or more of its projections.

Non-Loss Decomposition: Let R be a relation and $X_1, \ldots X_n$ be subsets of the attributes of R. Then the set of projections of R on $X_1, \ldots X_n$ is said to form a "Non-Loss decomposition" of R if R equals the join of all these projections; that is, R =PROJECT(R, X_1) JOIN PROJECT(R, X_2)… JOIN PROJECT(R, X_n).

Importance of Non-Loss Decomposition

As will be presented in the chapter on Normalization, it's often desirable to replace a relation by two or more of its projections. However, it's also often desirable to later JOIN these projections for data retrieval or other purposes. It's important that when the JOIN is done, we get the original relation back with no new rows added. This is what is assured by Non-Loss decomposition.

Non-Loss Decomposition Based on Functional Dependency

Inference 4.3.1: Let X,Y,Z be subsets of the attributes of a relation R, where each attribute is in at least one of these subsets. Then any row in R is also a row in PROJECT(R, X $\cup$ Y) JOIN PROJECT(R, X $\cup$ Z).

Note that X $\cup$ Y is the set of all the attributes in X and all those in Y; that is, it's the set union of X and Y.

The above inference states that we get all the rows of R – and possibly some additional rows – back when we do the decomposition and then the join as specified. Heath's Theorem adds a condition to ensure that we get R back with no additional rows.

Heath's Theorem (form 1): Let X, Y, and Z be subsets of the attributes of a relation, R, such that each attribute is in at least one of these subsets. If R satisfies the FD X→Y, then R = PROJECT(R, XUY) JOIN PROJECT(R, XUZ). That is, R is non-loss decomposable into its projections on XUY and XUZ.

Inference 4.3.2: Let R be a relation with attribute sets X and Y' such that there is an FD X→Y'. If we let Y=Y' - X and let Z consist of the attributes of R that aren't in X or Y, then each attribute in R appears in exactly one of these sets and – from Inference 4.1.4 – R satisfies the FD X→Y.

It follows from the above that there is no loss of applicability by requiring that the attribute sets have no attributes in common. Thus, we'll use the following statement of Heath's Theorem:

Heath's Theorem: Let X, Y, and Z be subsets of the attributes of a relation, R, such that each attribute is in exactly one of these sets. If R satisfies the FD X→Y, then R = PROJECT(R, XUY) JOIN PROJECT(R, XUZ). That is, R is non-loss decomposable into its projections on XUY and XUZ.

Inference 4.3.3: The converse of Heath's theorem is not true. That is, if R = PROJECT(R, XUY) JOIN PROJECT(R, XUZ) it doesn't necessarily follow that X→Y.

Note: Heath's theorem will be used for Normal Forms 2, 3 and Boyce-Codd to be covered later.

Non-Loss Decomposition Based on Multivalued Dependency

Fagin's Theorem: Let X, Y and Z be subsets of the attributes of a relation, R, such that each attribute is in exactly one of these subsets. Then R satisfies the MVD X→→Y|Z if and only if R=PROJECT(R, XUY) JOIN PROJECT(R, XUZ). That is, R is non-loss decomposable into its projections on XUY and XUZ.

Note: Fagin's theorem will be used for Normal Form 4 to be covered later.

Example 1: Heath's Theorem

Each row of the Instructors relation on the right contains the courses that each instructor has taught. Also included is the department that offers that course.

We can make the following observations about this relation:

{Course}→{Department}. That is, the attribute Department is functionally dependent on the attribute Course.

Instructors

Name	Course	Department
Wilson	Grammar I	English
Lenox	Algebra I	Math
Jones	Acct I	Business
Peterson	Algebra I	Math
Barret	Grammar I	English
Lenox	GenPhysics	Physics
Henson	AmHistory	History
Carter	French	Language

From Heath's Theorem it follows that Instructors = Project (Instructors, {Course, Department}) Join Project(Instructors, {Course, Name}). Hence the Instructors relation can be non-loss decomposed into the relations on the right.

Name	Course
Wilson	Grammar I
Lenox	Algebra I
Jones	Acct I
Peterson	Algebra I
Barret	Grammar I
Lenox	GenPhysics
Henson	AmHistory
Carter	French

Course	Department
Grammar I	English
Algebra I	Math
Acct I	Business
GenPhysics	Physics
AmHistory	History
French	Language

Example 2: Fagin's Theorem

A manufacturer produces two types of refrigerators: one with the freezer on top and one with the freezer on the bottom. They offer the refrigerators with the top freezer in both white and almond; the bottom freezer models are offered only in white. The combinations of size and color for each type appear in the Refrigerators relation on the right.

We observe that Freezer→→Size|Color. That is, Freezer multidetermines Size and Color.

Refrigerators

Freezer	Size	Color
Top	14.5	White
Top	18.5	White
Top	14.5	Almond
Top	18.5	Almond
Bottom	18.5	White
Bottom	22	White

From Fagin's Theorem it follows that Refrigerators = Project (Refrigerators, {Freezer, Size}) Join Project (Refrigerators, {Freezer, Color}). Hence the Refrigerators relation can be non-loss decomposed into the relations on the right.

Freezer	Size
Top	14.5
Top	18.5
Bottom	18.5
Bottom	22

Freezer	Color
Top	White
Top	Almond
Bottom	White

Independently Updateable Decomposition

In addition to being non-loss, another desirable property of a decomposition is that the resulting set of projections is "Independently Updateable" as defined next.

Independently Updateable: The set of projections in a non-loss decomposition is said to be "independently updateable" if the join of the projections never contains a violation of a functional dependency in the original relation. That is, there isn't any possibility that there could be values in a projection that – when joined with the other projections – could result in a violation of an FD in the resulting join.

Thus the values in each projection are not constrained by the values in the other projections except for referential integrity constraints. (As usual, any relationship between projections would require – by referential integrity – that every foreign key value in one relation match a candidate key value in the other.)

A practical consequence of having non-loss decompositions that are independently updateable is that each projection can be updated without having to ensure that the updated values wouldn't cause an FD violation in the join of the projections. Hence, when updating the values in one of the relations in the decomposition, one doesn't have to be concerned about the values in the other relations.

Next, we define a property that – in addition to being an intrinsically important feature by itself – can also be used to determine if a decomposition is independently updateable.

Dependency Preservation: A set of projections of a relation are said to be "dependency preserving" if all the functional dependencies in the original relation can be constructed from the FDs in the projections by using Armstrong's Axioms (see Section 4.1).

The following inference presents criteria for ensuring that a decomposition is independently updateable.

Inference 4.3.4: The projections that form a non-loss, dependency preserving decomposition are independently updateable.

Example 1: non-Independently Updateable Projections

This example is similar to one in reference [Ri]. In relation Seminar, an Attendee will attend a lecture with number LecNum at time Hour on the day of the seminar. Assume that the name Attendee is unique and that each lecture is given only at one time. The FDs in Seminar are LecNum→Hour, {Attendee, Hour}→LecNum, and {Attendee, LecNum}→Hour .

Seminar

Attendee	Hour	LecNum
Wilson	10:30	L02
Lenox	14:00	L08
Jones	09:00	L04
Lenox	10:30	L01
Peterson	14:00	L08

Consider the projections of Seminar to the right where Project1 has been updated by adding the italicized row. Project1 has one candidate key {LecNum, Attendee} and no non-trivial FDs; Project2 has candidate key LecNum and one FD LecNum→Hour. There are no apparent violations of FDs, however, doing the join does reveal a violation as shown below.

Project1

LecNum	Attendee
L02	Wilson
L08	Lenox
L04	Jones
L01	Lenox
L08	Peterson
L01	*Wilson*

Project2

LecNum	Hour
L02	10:30
L08	14:00
L04	09:00
L01	10:30

In the JOIN of the projections, we see that Wilson is scheduled to two lectures at the same time. This occurs because the FD {Attendee, Hour}→LecNum was not preserved in the decomposition. Thus the projections cannot be updated independently.

Seminar

Attendee	Hour	LecNum
Wilson	*10:30*	*L02*
Lenox	14:00	L08
Jones	09:00	L04
Lenox	10:30	L01
Peterson	14:00	L08
Wilson	*10:30*	*L01*

Example 2: Independently Updateable Projections

For relation Orders, the order with OrdNum is for customer with ID CustID and name CustNam where CustID (but not necessarily CustNam) is unique for each customer. Orders has the FDs: OrdNum →CustID, OrdNum→CustNam and OrdNum→{CustID, CustNam}, CustID →CustNam

Orders

OrdNum	CustID	CustNam
ON00100	CN0009	Wilco
ON00112	CN0025	Martel
ON00134	CN0009	Wilco
ON00126	CN0018	Apex
ON00135	CN0025	Martel

We'll show that the projections of Orders to the right are independently updateable by using Inference 4.3.4.

1. The only FD in Project1 is CustID →CustNam. The only FD in Project2 is OrdNum →CustID.

Project1

CustID	CustNam
CN0009	Wilco
CN0025	Martel
CN0018	Apex

Project2

OrdNum	CustID
ON00100	CN0009
ON00112	CN0025
ON00134	CN0009
ON00126	CN0018
ON00135	CN0025

By using the Armstrong transitivity axiom and OrdNum →CustID, CustID →CustNam we can construct OrdNum→CustNam. By the union axiom and the FDs OrdNum →CustID, OrdNum→CustNam we can deduce that OrdNum→ {CustID, CustNam}. Thus all the FDs in Orders can be constructed by using the FDs in the projections and Armstrong's Axioms. Therefore, by definition, the decomposition is dependency preserving.

2. Since CustID →CustNam we know from Heath's Theorem that the decomposition is non-loss.

Since the decomposition is non-loss and dependency preserving, it follows from Inference 4.3.4 that the projections are independently updateable.

Section 4.4 Join Dependence

The dependencies discussed thus far – functional and multivalued – have led to decompositions that involve replacing a relation by two of its projections. However, reference [ABU] shows that it's possible to have relations with non-loss decompositions that are not the result of forming successive two projection non-loss decompositions. The concept of Join Dependency, then, pertains to defining a dependency and the associated decomposition for relations of this type.

Join Dependency (JD): Let R be a relation and let $X_1, X_2 \ldots X_n$ be subsets of the attributes of R. Then R is said to satisfy the JD $*(X_1, X_2 \ldots X_n)$ if and only if R is equal to the join of its projections on $X_1, X_2 \ldots X_n$. Alternatively, R is said to satisfy the JD $*(X_1, X_2 \ldots X_n)$ if and only if the projections of R on $X_1, X_2 \ldots X_n$ form a non-loss decomposition of R.

It follows that ascertaining whether subsets of the attributes $X_1, \ldots X_n$ of a relation R satisfy JD $*(X_1, X_2 \ldots X_n)$ entails determining if their projections form a non-loss decomposition of R. To this end, we present the following algorithm and associated theorem from reference [UI].

Algorithm 4.4.1 – Determining if a decomposition is non-loss: Let R be a relation with attributes $A_1, \ldots A_m$ where F is a minimal cover for the functional dependencies in R, and $R_1, \ldots R_n$ form a decomposition of R.

First, construct a table with m columns and n rows where, as in the preceding, m is the number of attributes in R and n is the number of components in the decomposition of R. Column k will correspond to A_k and row i to R_i. In row i and column k put the symbol a_k if A_k is in R_i. If not, put the symbol b_{ik} there.

Then repeat the following for each FD $X \rightarrow Y$ in the minimal cover, F, until some row in the table is $a_1 \ldots a_m$ or until no more changes can be made.

For an FD $X \rightarrow Y$ in F: If there are two rows that are equal in all the columns for the attributes of X, then make the symbols in these rows equal in the columns for the attributes of Y. That is, if one symbol is a_k make the other a_k; If the symbols are b_{ik} and b_{hk}, then either make them both b_{ik} or make them both b_{hk}.

Furthermore, when changing a symbol such as b_{ik}, change all occurrences of the symbol in the column. For example, if we are changing b_{ik} to a_k or to b_{hk} make the same change for all occurrences of b_{ik} in the column. Note that it's possible for b_{ik} to occur more than once in a column because a symbol such as b_{hk} may have been changed to b_{ik} by a previous step of the algorithm.

After modifying the table as above, the decomposition is non-loss if and only if some row is $a_1 \ldots a_m$.

Theorem 4.4.2: Algorithm 4.4.1 correctly determines if a decomposition is non-loss.

Example
A Non-loss Decomposition that's not the Result of Successive Two Projection Non-loss Decompositions.
(This is a specific case of a general example that appears in [ABU].)

Each row of relation R contains information about a course that will be offered in the coming semester. The set of attributes is {InstID, Name, Time, Loc, Dept, Course} where: InstID = an instructor ID, Name = instructor's last name, Time = time the course is offered, Loc = room/building, Dept = Department, Course = the course name. The following is a minimal cover for the functional dependencies:

InstID→Name, Course →Dept, {InstID, Time}→Loc, {Loc, Time}→Course, {Loc, Time}→InstID.

Define 3 subsets of the attributes as: INLD = {InstID, Name, Loc, Dept}, ITLC = {InstID, Time, Loc, Course}, and NTDC ={Name, Time, Dept, Course}

First, we'll use Algorithm 4.4.1 to show that the projections of R on INLD, ITLC, and NTDC form a non-loss decomposition of R

The initial table for Algorithm 4.4.1 is on the right. Using Algorithm 4.4.1 with InstID→Name changes b_{22} to a_2. Similarly, Course →Dept

	InstID	Name	Time	Loc	Dept	Course
INLD	a_1	a_2	b_{13}	a_4	a_5	b_{16}
ITLC	a_1	b_{22}	a_3	a_4	b_{25}	a_6
NTDC	b_{31}	a_2	a_3	b_{34}	a_5	a_6

changes b_{25} to a_5. The table resulting from these changes is presented below.

Since the second row is $a_1 \ldots a_6$ we can terminate the algorithm. We deduce from Theorem 4.4.2 that the projections on the attribute sets

	InstID	Name	Time	Loc	Dept	Course
INLD	a_1	a_2	b_{13}	a_4	a_5	b_{16}
ITLC	a_1	a_2	a_3	a_4	a_5	a_6
NTDC	b_{31}	a_2	a_3	b_{34}	a_5	a_6

INLD, ITLC and NTDC form a non-loss decomposition and thus – by definition – R satisfies the JD *(INLD, ITLC, NTDC).

Next, we'll show that the decomposition formed by the projections of INLD, ITLC, and NTDC isn't the result of successive two projection non-loss decompositions:

If the projections of INLD, ITLC, and NTDC were the result of non-loss two projection decompositions, then there would be a relation, S, such that one of the following cases would be true:

Case 1) Project(R, INLD) and S form a non-loss decomposition of R; also, Project(R, ITLC) and Project(R, NTDC) form a non-loss decomposition of S.
or Case 2) Like Case 1 but switching ITLC and INLD.
or Case 3) Like Case 1 but switching NTLC and INLD.

For Case 1 the projections of ITLC, NTDC must form a non-loss decomposition of S so the attributes in S are all the attributes in ITLC and in NTDC which are all the attributes in R. Since S is a projection of R with the same attributes, S = R. This implies that the projections of ITLC and NTDC form a non-loss decomposition of R. Initializing the table for Algorithm 4.4.1 yields the relation below.

Using Algorithm 4.4.1, the FD Course→Dept changes b_{15} to a_5 resulting as in the table below; No other FDs have any effect.

	InstID	Name	Time	Loc	Dept	Course
ITLC	a_1	b_{12}	a_3	a_4	b_{15}	a_6
NTDC	b_{21}	a_2	a_3	b_{24}	a_5	a_6

Since no row is $a_1 \ldots a_6$, the projections of ITLC and NTDC don't form a non-loss decomposition of R and hence Case 1 can't occur. In a

	InstID	Name	Time	Loc	Dept	Course
ITLC	a_1	b_{12}	a_3	a_4	a_5	a_6
NTDC	b_{21}	a_2	a_3	b_{24}	a_5	a_6

similar way we could show that Case 2 and Case 3 couldn't occur.

Thus, the decomposition formed by the projections of INLD, ITLC, and NTDC isn't the result of successive two projection non-loss decompositions.

The next two inferences reveal some characteristics of joins of projections.

Inference 4.4.3: Let R be a relation and let X_1, X_2 ... X_n be subsets of its attributes. Then any row in the projection of R on the union of these subsets is also a row in the joins of the individual projections. That is, any row in Project (R, $X_1 \cup$ ... X_n) is also a row in the Project(R, X_1) JOIN Project(R, X_2)... JOIN Project(R, X_n).

The following is just a special case of the inference above and shows that for attribute subsets whose union contains all the attributes of a relation R, the joins of the projections on those subsets contains all the rows in R. Thus, a decomposition of this type is non-loss if taking these joins produces no extra rows.

Inference 4.4.4: Let R be a relation and let X_1, X_2 ... X_n be subsets of its attributes such that every attribute in R appears in at least one of these subsets. Then any row in R is also a row in the joins of the individual projections. That is, any row in R is also a row in the Project(R, X_1) JOIN Project(R, X_2)... JOIN Project(R, X_n).

Inference 4.4.5: Let R be a relation and let X_1, X_2 ... X_n be subsets of its attributes where one of the subsets, X_i, is the set of all the attributes in R. Then R satisfies JD *(X_1, X_2 ... X_n).

In light of the preceding inference we can now make the following definition.

Trivial Join Dependency: A JD *(X_1, X_2 ... X_n) is called a trivial JD if and only if one of the subsets, X_i, is the set of all the attributes in R.

The following inference shows how JDs are, in a sense, a generalization of MVDs.

Inference 4.4.6: Let the attributes of a relation R be partitioned into subsets X, Y, Z such that each attribute is in exactly one of these subsets. Then R satisfies JD*(X $\cup$ Y, X $\cup$ Z) if and only if X$\rightarrow\rightarrow$Y$|$Z.

Non-Loss Decomposition Based on Join Dependency

To reiterate: Some relations cannot be non-loss decomposed into two projections but can be non-loss decomposed into three or more. Join Dependency is the condition that ensures this non-loss decomposition.

Join dependency and the associated decomposition complete the topic of dependency and decomposition. But unlike functional and multivalued dependencies, JDs are themselves defined in terms of decomposability and are, in practice, very difficult to discern.

However, a common condition is presented in Chapter 5 (see "A condition for guaranteeing 5NF") that can eliminate the need to check for join dependencies.

Note: Join dependencies are used for Normal Form 5 to be discussed later.

Example: A Specific Instance of a Non-loss Decomposition into 3 Components

Each row of relation R on the right contains information about a course that will be offered in the coming semester. The set of attributes is {InstID, Name, Time,

R

InstID	Name	Time	Loc	Dept	Course
I017	Jones	15:00	500/Main	Math	Calculus I
I017	Jones	16:00	500/Main	Physics	Optics I
I065	Wilson	16:00	300/Annex	English	Grammar

Loc, Dept, Course} where: InstID = an instructor ID, Name = instructor's last name, Time = time the course is offered, Loc = room/building, Dept = Department, Course = the course name.

In the preceding example, we showed that this relation is non-loss decomposable into R_1, R_2, and R_3 as defined below. We also proved that this decomposition couldn't be constructed from successive two projection non-loss decompositions. Here, we merely demonstrate that the instance of R with the given rows is non-loss decomposable into relations R_1, R_2, and R_3.

Let R_1 = Project(R, {InstID, Name, Loc, Dept}) as on the right.

R_1

InstID	Name	Loc	Dept
I017	Jones	500/Main	Math
I017	Jones	500/Main	Physics
I065	Wilson	300/Annex	English

Let R_2 = Project(R, {InstID, Time, Loc, Course}) as on the right.

R_2

InstID	Time	Loc	Course
I017	15:00	500/Main	Calculus I
I017	16:00	500/Main	Optics I
I065	16:00	300/Annex	Grammar

Let R_3 = Project(R, {Name, Time, Dept, Course}) as on the right.

R_3

Name	Time	Dept	Course
Jones	15:00	Math	Calculus I
Jones	16:00	Physics	Optics I
Wilson	16:00	English	Grammar

Then the result of R_1 Join R_2 is the relation to the right. This has all the rows in the original relation plus two extra (which we've italicized).

R_1 Join R_2

InstID	Name	Time	Loc	Dept	Course
I017	Jones	15:00	500/Main	Math	Calculus I
I017	*Jones*	*16:00*	*500/Main*	*Math*	*Optics I*
I017	*Jones*	*15:00*	*500/Main*	*Physics*	*Calculus I*
I017	Jones	16:00	500/Main	Physics	Optics I
I065	Wilson	16:00	300/Annex	English	Grammar

Finally, the result of (R_1 Join R_2) Join R_3 is the relation to the right. This final Join eliminates the extra rows and yields the original relation, thereby demonstrating that

(R_1 Join R_2) Join R_3

InstID	Name	Time	Loc	Dept	Course
I017	Jones	15:00	500/Main	Math	Calculus I
I017	Jones	16:00	500/Main	Physics	Optics I
I065	Wilson	16:00	300/Annex	English	Grammar

for the given rows, R is non-loss decomposable into R_1, R_2, and R_3.

Chapter 5
Normalization

As described in Chapter 1, we use tables to model real world entities in a relational database. However, there may be problems that arise in the database if the tables are improperly designed. By the "improper design" of a table we loosely mean that its attributes shouldn't all be in one table together. Now that we've discussed such topics as projection, join, dependence and decomposition, we can specifically address what is meant by proper design or "normalization." Further, we'll describe procedures for replacing existing problematic tables with normalized ones.

Overview

A table that is not designed "properly" can cause problems such as:
- Redundancies that waste space.
- Update Anomalies that make it difficult to update the database by inserting, altering or deleting data.

The rules for proper design have been formalized into increasingly stringent levels of criteria called "Normal Forms" that progressively avoid more and more redundancies and update anomalies. Since the criteria are increasingly restrictive, a table normalized to any level of Normal Form is also normalized to all the previous levels.

The levels of normal forms are:
First Normal Form (1NF)
Second Normal Form (2NF)
Third Normal Form (3NF)
Boyce-Codd Normal Form (BCNF)
Fourth Normal Form (4NF)
Fifth Normal Form (5NF) also called Projection Join Normal Form (PJNF)

Normalization to a certain level refers to the process of replacing a table that does not satisfy the criteria for that level by tables that do. When all the tables in a database are at a certain level of normalization, then we say that the database is normalized to that level.

Attainability of Normal Forms

We'll see that any table that satisfies the criteria for a relation is, by definition, normalized to 1NF. Further, it has been proven [Fa2] that any relation can be decomposed into all the higher normal forms. That is, all the normal forms listed above are attainable. More specifically: 2NF, 3NF, BCNF and 4NF can be achieved by successive replacement of a relation with two of its projections to form a non-loss decomposition; 5NF can be attained by successive replacement of a relation with two or more of its projections to form a non-loss decomposition.

This chapter will discuss each of these normal forms in order.

Section 5.1 First Normal Form

By definition, a table that's a relation as defined in Chapter 1 is in First Normal Form; hence, this section repeats some of the material from that Chapter. We then proceed to describe a generalization of a non single valued attribute called a "repeating group." Finally, we discuss how to get a relation from tables with these problematic groups. The task of attaining 1NF is, of course, dependent on the original table; similarly, the structure of the resulting relation can affect how difficult it will be to get to higher normal forms.

First Normal Form: A table is in First Normal Form (1NF) if and only if it is a relation.

For convenience, we restate the definitions for Single Valued Attribute and Relation from Chapter 1:

Single Valued Attribute: An attribute that can only assume a single value from its domain – not a list of values.

Relation: A Table satisfying the following rules.

1) There is no order to the rows. That is, the table can be represented with the rows in any order without changing its meaning.
2) There is no order to the columns.
3) No two rows are the same. At least one attribute value must be different for any two rows.
4) All attributes are single valued. Namely, the value on any row for any column in the table is either the null value or a single value from that column's domain – not a list of values.

The first 3 rules are generally straightforward and therefore we'll concentrate on the last rule for the remainder of this section. That is, we'll consider tables where rules 1 – 3, but not 4, hold and discuss ways to restructure these tables to satisfy rule 4. Note that we're implicitly assuming that there's at least one single valued attribute and that the set of all single valued attributes is a super key.

We begin by considering a generalization of non-single valued attributes called a "repeating group" that often quite naturally appears.

Repeating Group: A Repeating Group is a set of "interrelated" non-single valued attributes such that for a given row there can be many group values where the relation description is true on that row. Note that if there is only one attribute in the set, the repeating group is simply a non-single valued attribute.

If $G = \{G_1, \ldots G_n\}$ is a set of non-single valued attributes, then we'll call a set of values $G' = \{G_1', \ldots G_n'\}$ an instance of G.

By "interrelated" we mean that for a given row, a value for an attribute in the group may only be valid with certain values of the other attributes in G. That is, it's possible for the values of two different attributes in G to each appear in a valid instance of G on some row but not appear in the same instance. One can only confirm that a set of attributes is interrelated by understanding the meaning of the attributes in the relation description.

In the following, let A be the set of attributes that are not in a repeating group.

On the right we represent a row of a table with one Repeating Group $G = \{G_1, \ldots G_n\}$ where this set of A values is valid with each set of G values.

A	G
One set of A values.	Multiple sets of G values

Also it's possible for a table to have more than one repeating group. If a table has two repeating groups, G and H, we can represent one row of this table as below. This set of A values is valid with each set of G values (or instance of G) paired with each set of H values.

A	G	H
One set of A values.	Multiple sets of G values	Multiple sets of H values

Example 1: A Table with One Single Attribute Repeating Group

On the right, we represent the Emp/Proj table: The employee with the indicated last name (we'll assume last names are unique) has worked on the project with ID ProjID. This table has the repeating group {ProjID} consisting of one non-single valued attribute.

Emp/Proj

LName	ProjID
Wilson	P1289
	P7650
Mason	P7650
Johnson	P1289
	P2098
	P1654

Example 2: A Table with One Multi-Attribute Repeating Group

In the Orders table, each order with OrderNum for a customer with ID CustID specifies the products identified by ProdID with the corresponding Quantity. There is only one customer for each order. This table has the repeating group {ProdID, Quantity}.

Orders

OrderNum	CustID	ProdID	Quantity
ON16	C34	P18	3
		P21	1
		P14	4
ON23	C25	P09	6
		P18	1

Note that CustID – though intuitively related to the other attributes in the group – isn't in the group because it's single valued. The other attributes are interrelated because for a given row it's possible for an attribute to have a value that isn't valid with some other attribute value: For example, P18 isn't valid with 1 on the row with ON16. Even if this didn't occur in the example, we know from the meaning of {ProdID, Quantity} that it could occur.

Example 3: A Table with Two Repeating Groups

On the right, we represent the Employees table: The employee with LName (assume LName is unique) currently has the indicated JobTitle, has a child with first name Child, and has worked on the project with ID ProjID. This table has the repeating groups {Child} and {ProjID}.

Note that {Child, ProjID} is not a repeating group because Child and ProjID are not interrelated. That is, we know from their meaning that a value

Employees

LName	JobTitle	Child	ProjID
Wilson	Analyst	Wanda	P12
		William	P76
		Wendy	
Mason	Programmer	Matthew	P76
Johnson	Engineer	James	P12
		Janet	P20
			P16
			P06

of Child is valid with any value of ProjID. For example, Wanda is valid with both P12 and P76 on the row with LName Wilson.

<u>Forming a relation from a table that has a repeating group.</u>

If we want a table with repeating groups to be a relation – and thus in 1NF – we must represent it in such a way that all attributes are single valued. First, we'll describe how to implement this representation by adding columns to the original table. However, we'll see that this approach causes other problems and should be avoided. Next, we'll discuss the method of adding rows. This works well and doesn't introduce any new problems. Finally, we point out that if there is more than one repeating group in the original table, they should be separated into different tables before forming relations.

On the right, we represent a row of a table with one repeating group that has K sets of values for a set of A values where A is the set of all the attributes not in G.

A	G
A values	1st set of G values
	...
	Kth set of G values

Add Columns Method:

We replace the G column above by new columns containing all the values of the repeating group. As we'll see, this method should be avoided; we merely present it here for completeness. Let T be a table with one repeating group $G = \{G_1, \ldots G_n\}$ and let A be the set of all the remaining attributes. Further, let M be our estimate of the maximum number of sets of values of G that can occur for any row. Let $G1 = \{G1_1, \ldots G1_n\}, \ldots GM = \{GM_1, \ldots GM_n\}$ each be a set of n unique attribute names corresponding to the set of attributes $G = \{G_1, \ldots G_n\}$. Next, replace the original table by one with attribute sets A, G1, ... GM.

On the right, we represent a row of the revised table with the repeating group implemented by adding columns.

A	G1	...	GM
A values	G1 values	...	GM values

All the attributes are now single valued and the revised table is a relation and therefore in 1NF. However, we must estimate the maximum number (M above) of attribute sets that will be needed. If the estimate is too large, nulls will be created and space will be wasted; if it is too small, there won't be any place to put some of the data. This implementation should also be avoided because it can make the predicate, – that is, the relation description – unnecessarily complicated.

Add Rows Method:

Replace each row in the original table by rows consisting of the values for the single valued attributes in the original row plus one set of values for the repeating group from the original row. In this way, create a row for each set of values in the repeating group.

On the right, we represent the rows of a relation that resulted from replacing one row in the original table. If the repeating group had K sets of G values for these A values, then the original row is replaced by K rows.

A	G
A values	1st set of G values
...	...
A values	Kth set of G values

Example 1: Forming a Relation from a Table with One Single Attribute Repeating Group

On the right, we represent the Emp/Proj table: The employee LName has worked on the projects with IDs ProjID. This table has the non-single valued attribute ProjID that forms the repeating group {ProjID}. (We'll assume that last names are unique.)

Emp/Proj

LName	ProjID
Wilson	P12
	P76
Mason	P76
Johnson	P12
	P20
	P16

Using the Add Columns Method on the Emp/Proj table results in the relation to the right with the candidate key LName. The estimated maximum number of projects is 4 and the indicated attributes correspond to ProjID. We reiterate that this method should be avoided and the following method used.

LName	ProjIDa	ProjIDb	ProjIDc	ProjIDd
Wilson	P12	P76	Null	Null
Mason	P76	Null	Null	Null
Johnson	P12	P20	P16	Null

Using the Add Rows Method on the initial Emp/Proj table yields the relation to the right. The candidate key for this relation is {LName, ProjID}.

LName	ProjID
Wilson	P12
Wilson	P76
Mason	P76
Johnson	P12
Johnson	P20
Johnson	P16

Example 2: Forming a Relation from a Table with One Multi-Attribute Repeating Group

On the right, we represent the Orders table: Each Order Number is for one customer identified by CustID and specifies product ProdID with the corresponding UnitPrice and Quantity. This table has the repeating group {ProdID, UnitPrice, Quantity}.

Orders

ONum	CustID	ProdID	UnitPrice	Quantity
ON16	CN34	P18	348.00	3
		P25	1765.00	1
		P14	145.00	4
ON23	CN25	P09	85.00	6
		P21	1765.00	1

The relation formed by using the Add Rows method on the Orders table appears to the right. The candidate key for this relation is {ONum, ProdID}.

ONum	CustID	ProdID	UnitPrice	Quantity
ON16	CN34	P18	348.00	3
ON16	CN34	P25	1765.00	1
ON16	CN34	P14	145.00	4
ON23	CN25	P09	85.00	6
ON23	CN25	P21	1765.00	1

– Section 5.1: First Normal Form –

Forming relations from a table that has more than one repeating group.

First we'll show that for a table with more than one repeating group, it's not advisable to merely do the add rows method successively until the repeating groups are eliminated.

On the right, we represent a row of a table with two repeating groups, G and H, that have K and L sets of values respectively on a row with these A values.

A row from Table 1

A	G	H
A values	1st set of G values ... Kth set of G values	1st set of H values ... Lth set of H values

Doing the add rows method for G and again for H we obtain this set of K x L rows to replace the original row. In addition to producing many rows, this method is also problematic because it can lead to "Multivalued Dependencies" which we'll see later are a violation of 4NF.

A	G	H
A values	1st set of G values	1st set of H values
...	...	...
A values	Kth set of G values	1st set of H values
...	...	...
A values	1st set of G values	Lth set of L values
...	...	...
A values	Kth set of G values	Lth set of L values

Rather than doing the add rows method successively on a table with multiple repeating groups, it's advisable to first form new tables that each has only one repeating group. In the case of two repeating groups as above, we could first replace Table 1 with Table 1H and Table 1G as follows:

One scheme for separating the two repeating groups into different tables is to first create the table on the right where A is the same set of attributes as in the original table

A row from Table 1G

A	G
A values	1st set of G values ... Kth set of G values

Recalling from the beginning of this section that A is a super key, we let A' be a subset of A that's a candidate key for Table 1 and form Table 1H with sets A' and H. Here we present a row from this table. (Note that if A is a candidate key, then A'=A.)

A row from Table 1H

A'	H
A' values	1st set of H values ... Lth set of H values

Using the add rows method on Table 1G we obtain a relation that only models the repeating group G, not H. The rows that replace the row in Table 1G are presented here.

A row from Relation 1G

A	G
A values	1st set of G values
A values	...
A values	Kth set of G values

Similarly, we use the add rows method on Table 1H to get a relation that doesn't have the set of attributes G. The rows of a relation that replace a row in Table 1H appear to the right.

Thus we've replaced Table 1, which isn't a relation and has two repeating groups with the two relations 1G and 1H.

A row from Relation 1H

A'	H
A' values	1st set of H values
A' values	...
A' values	Lth set of H values

We summarize the approach for separating repeating groups as:

Note 5.1.1: Don't resolve more than one repeating group into a single relation. If a table has more than one repeating group, first replace it by tables that each has only one repeating group. Then form a relation from each of the resulting tables by using the add rows method.

Example: Forming Relations from a Table with Two Repeating Groups

On the right, we represent the Emp table: The employee with LName currently has the indicated JobTitle; has children with the indicated first names and has worked on the projects with IDs ProjID. (We'll assume that employee last names are unique.)

LName is the candidate key for this table and there are two repeating groups {Child} and {ProjID}.

Emp

LName	JobTitle	Child	ProjID
Wilson	Analyst	Wanda	P04
		William	P23
		Wendy	
Mason	Programmer	Matthew	P23
Johnson	Engineer	James	P04
		Janet	P15
			P46

If we were to resolve the two repeating groups in table Emp with one relation, we would obtain the relation to the right. This approach is not recommended; we'll see in Section 5.4, that this relation violates "fourth normal form."

LName	JobTitle	Child	Project
Wilson	Analyst	Wanda	P04
Wilson	Analyst	Wanda	P23
Wilson	Analyst	William	P04
Wilson	Analyst	William	P23
Wilson	Analyst	Wendy	P04
Wilson	Analyst	Wendy	P23
Mason	Programmer	Matthew	P23
Johnson	Engineer	James	P04
Johnson	Engineer	James	P15
Johnson	Engineer	James	P46
Johnson	Engineer	Janet	P04
Johnson	Engineer	Janet	P15
Johnson	Engineer	Janet	P46

As stated in Note 5.1.1 at the end of the previous section, it's better to first separate the repeating groups into two tables and then make each table into a relation.

This approach is demonstrated in the rest of this example.

On the right, we represent tables that result from separating the two repeating groups in the Emp table: The Emp/Child table has the repeating group {Child}; the Emp/Proj table has the repeating group {ProjID}. Note that we've just included the candidate key LName in Emp/Proj and not the super key {LName, JobTitle}.

Emp/Child

LName	JobTitle	Child
Wilson	Analyst	Wanda
		William
		Wendy
Mason	Programmer	Matthew
Johnson	Engineer	James
		Janet

Emp/Proj

LName	ProjID
Wilson	P04
	P23
Mason	P23
Johnson	P04
	P15
	P46

Here we represent relations resulting from using the replace rows method on the Emp/Child and Emp/Proj tables respectively.

LName	JobTitle	Child
Wilson	Analyst	Wanda
Wilson	Analyst	William
Wilson	Analyst	Wendy
Mason	Programmer	Matthew
Johnson	Engineer	James
Johnson	Engineer	Janet

LName	ProjID
Wilson	P04
Wilson	P23
Mason	P23
Johnson	P04
Johnson	P15
Johnson	P46

Section 5.2 Second Normal Form

For the following, recall that every relation is in 1NF and that an informational attribute is an attribute that is not part of any candidate key.

By the definition of candidate key, we know that every informational attribute for a table in 1NF is functionally dependent on every candidate key. Second Normal Form further requires that every informational attribute is functionally dependent only on whole candidate keys – never just a part of one.

Second Normal Form (2NF): A relation is in Second Normal Form if and only if every informational attribute is fully functionally dependent on all candidate keys.

Inference 5.2.1: A relation is in 2NF if and only if there is no informational attribute that is functionally dependent on just part of a candidate key.

Update Anomalies When a Relation is not in 2NF:

Insert: To add a partial candidate key determinant value and the corresponding dependent informational attribute value, a row must be added. However, there may be no primary key value for which the row would be valid. Thus, there would be no way to record the fact that this informational attribute value corresponds to this partial candidate key value.

Delete: If the last row containing a specific value for a partial candidate key is deleted, the fact that the informational attribute value on that row corresponds to that partial candidate key value is lost. This correspondence may be significant apart from the appearance of these values on the deleted row.

Update: To update a value for an informational attribute that depends on a partial candidate key, it would be necessary to update it in every row that the corresponding partial candidate key value appears.

Normalization Procedure:

As with all the higher normal forms – 2NF through 5NF – normalization will be accomplished by successive non-loss decomposition. We'll continue to replace a relation that isn't in 2NF with non-loss decompositions until all the relations that replace the original are in 2NF. Heath's Theorem provides the basis for the decompositions that attain 2NF.

Starting with the relation that's not in 2NF, repeat steps 1 and 2 below until all the replacement relations from step 2 are in 2NF:

1) Let Y be the set of all the informational attributes that are each functionally dependent on some partial candidate key, X. Let Z be all the attributes that are not in X or Y.

2) Replace the relation by the two relations formed by its projections on X ∪ Y and X ∪ Z.

Since X → Y, the projections on X ∪ Y and X ∪ Z satisfy the requirements of Heath's Theorem and hence form a non-loss decomposition of the original relation.

Example 1: Normalizing to 2NF

For this relation, the order with ONum is for the customer with ID CustID. The product with ProdID on this order has the agreed upon price UnitPrice each for Quantity units. The candidate key for this relation is

Orders

ONum	CustID	ProdID	UnitPrice	Quantity
ON16	CN34	P18	348.00	3
ON16	CN34	P21	1765.00	1
ON16	CN34	P14	145.00	4
ON23	CN25	P09	85.00	6
ON23	CN25	P21	1765.00	1

{ONum, ProdID}; however, CustID is an informational attribute that is fully functionally dependent on ONum which is just part of the candidate key. Thus the Orders relation is not in 2NF.

Following the normalization procedure for 2NF, we replace the Orders relation with the following two relations that are both in 2NF:

ONum	CustID
ON16	CN34
ON23	CN25

ONum	ProdID	UnitPrice	Quantity
ON16	P18	348.00	3
ON16	P21	1765.00	1
ON16	P14	145.00	4
ON23	P09	85.00	6
ON23	P21	1765.00	1

Example 2: A non-informational attribute not fully dependent on a candidate key.

The purpose of this example is to show that there can be an attribute that is not fully dependent on a candidate key; however, the relation can still be in 2NF because the attribute is not informational. This example is a variation of one that appeared in reference [UI].

In the following relation a company breaks their sales area into regions that are each associated with a region code – RegCode. Assume that RegCodes are within cities. That is, no two cities have the same RegCode; however, there may be many RegCodes within a city.

In this relation {City, StreetAddress} and {StreetAddress, RegCode} are both candidate keys. City is dependent on RegCode and thus is not fully functionally dependent on the candidate key {StreetAddress, RegCode}. Nonetheless, this relation is in 2NF because City is part of a candidate key and therefore is not an informational attribute.

City	StreetAddress	RegCode
Bellevue, OH	4597 State Rd.	R06
Findley, IN	601 Prospect Ave.	R20
Bellevue, OH	17649 Lancaster St.	R06
Treelawn, MI	5699 Wilson Ct.	R27
Findley, IN	9852 Princeton Blvd.	R18

Section 5.3 Third Normal Form

As we've seen, 2NF requires that informational attributes be fully functionally dependent on every candidate key; 3NF further requires that they are fully functionally dependent only on candidate keys. After a basic discussion of 3NF, we'll turn to the concept of independently updateable decompositions as defined in Section 4.3 and see that the result of the basic procedure for attaining 3NF may not have this important property. However, there's another procedure that always produces an independently updateable decomposition in 3NF – something we can't guarantee for the normal forms higher than third.

Third Normal Form (3NF): A relation is in Third Normal Form if and only if every determinant of an informational attribute in a non trivial full functional dependency is a candidate key.

Inference 5.3.1: A relation that's in 3NF is also in 2NF.

The next two inferences contain minor differences and are equivalent definitions of 3NF:

Inference 5.3.2: A relation is in Third Normal Form if and only if every determinant of an informational attribute in a non trivial functional dependency is a super key.

The following allows the dependent in the functional dependency to contain more than one attribute.

Inference 5.3.3: A relation is in Third Normal Form if and only if every determinant of a set of informational attributes in a non trivial functional dependency is a super key.

The inference below provides a condition for deciding that a relation isn't in 3NF.

Inference 5.3.4: A relation is not in 3NF if there is an informational attribute, A, that's fully functionally dependent on a set of attributes, X, that isn't a candidate key and A isn't an attribute in X.

Update Anomalies When a Relation is not in 3NF:

– Insert: To add a non candidate key determinant value and the corresponding dependent informational attribute value, a row must be added. But there may be no candidate key value for which the row would be valid and thus no way to record that this attribute value corresponds to this non candidate key value.

– Delete: If the last row containing a specific value for a non candidate key determinant is deleted, the fact that the dependent informational attribute value on that row corresponds to the non candidate key value is lost. This correspondence may be significant apart from the appearance of these values on the deleted row.

– Update: To update the value for an informational attribute that depends on a non candidate key determinant, one must update it in every row that the corresponding non candidate key value appears.

Normalization Procedure:

As in the procedure for attaining 2NF, we'll use Heath's Theorem to replace relations that are not in 3NF with non loss decompositions until all the relations that replace the original are in 3NF.

Starting with a relation that's not in 3NF, repeat steps 1 and 2 below until all the replacement relations from step 2 are in 3NF:

1) Let Y be the set of all the informational attributes that are each fully functionally dependent on a set of attributes, X, that isn't a candidate key and has no attributes in common with Y. Let Z be all the attributes that aren't in X or Y.

2) Replace the relation by the two relations formed by its projections on X ∪ Y and X ∪ Z.

Since X → Y, the projections on X ∪ Y and X ∪ Z satisfy the requirements of Heath's Theorem and hence form a non loss decomposition of the original relation.

This procedure doesn't ensure that the result is independently updateable; however, next we'll present a method – though more difficult – that does guarantee this.

Example 1: The Normalization Procedure Results in non Independently Updateable Projections.

A company sells and services large, complex equipment. Service requests are tracked in the ServiceRequests relation where a request with number ServNum involves equipment EqNum for customer CustID located in company region CustReg. ServOrg is the organiza-

ServiceRequests

ServNum	EqNum	CustID	CustReg	ServOrg
SN10	EQ08	CN09	CR35	Org50
SN12	EQ16	CN25	CR28	Org22
SN34	EQ05	CN09	CR35	Org71
SN26	EQ05	CN18	CR11	Org33
SN35	EQ16	CN25	CR28	Org22

tion within the company that has responsibility for servicing the equipment. ServOrg is dependent both on the equipment and the region in which the customer is located. The only candidate key is ServNum; all the other attributes are informational. Since there is no partial candidate key, this relation is in 2NF. However, there are full functional dependencies CustID→CustReg, {EqNum, CustReg}→ServOrg and {EqNum, CustID}→ServOrg and thus ServiceRequests is not in 3NF.

Resolving the dependency CustID→CustReg yields the following relations to replace ServiceRequests.

CustID	CustReg
CN09	CR35
CN25	CR28
CN18	CR11

ServNum	EqNum	CustID	ServOrg
SN10	EQ08	CN09	Org50
SN12	EQ16	CN25	Org22
SN34	EQ05	CN09	Org71
SN26	EQ05	CN18	Org33
SN35	EQ16	CN25	Org22

Next, resolving the dependency {EqNum, CustID}→ServOrg in the relation on the above right results in the following 3NF relations:

A

CustID	CustReg
CN09	CR35
CN25	CR28
CN18	CR11

B

EqNum	CustID	ServOrg
EQ08	CN09	Org50
EQ16	CN25	Org22
EQ05	CN09	Org71
EQ05	CN18	Org33

C

ServNum	EqNum	CustID
SN10	EQ08	CN09
SN12	EQ16	CN25
SN34	EQ05	CN09
SN26	EQ05	CN18
SN35	EQ16	CN25

The preceding demonstrates the use of the normalization procedure to obtain relations in 3NF to replace the original that was in 2NF. In the following, we show that the result isn't independently updateable.

Consider what happens if Customer CN18 moves to region CR35. Relation A updated with this new value of CustReg is presented on the right. The result of taking the Join of the updated relation A on the right with relations B and C above is presented below.

CustID	CustReg
CN09	CR35
CN25	CR28
CN18	*CR35*

A Join B Join C

ServNum	EqNum	CustID	CustReg	ServOrg
SN10	EQ08	CN09	CR35	Org50
SN12	EQ16	CN25	CR28	Org22
SN34	EQ05	CN09	CR35	*Org71*
SN26	EQ05	CN18	CR35	*Org33*
SN35	EQ16	CN25	CR28	Org22

We know this join is non-Loss from the discussion of the 3NF decomposition procedure. However, the values for {EqNum, CustReg} are the same on rows SN34 and SN26 while the values for ServOrg are different. Thus the FD {EqNum, CustReg}→ServOrg has been lost and we cannot independently update the decomposition consisting of the relations A, B and C.

Independently Updateable Decomposition into Third Normal Form

As discussed in Section 4.3, in addition to being non loss, another important property of decomposition is that the resulting set of projections is "Independently Updateable." It turns out that it's always possible to attain a non loss, independently updateable decomposition of a relation in 3NF as discussed in the remainder of this section. If further normalization results in a loss of the independently updateable property, one may – with good reason – decide to stop the normalization process at 3NF.

For convenience we repeat the definition of minimal cover from Section 4.1.

Minimal Cover for a Set of Dependencies of a Relation: A set of functional dependencies, F, for some relation, R, is said to be a "Minimal Cover" for all the FDs in R if:

1. For every FD $X \rightarrow A$ in F, A contains just one attribute.
2. Every FD $X \rightarrow A$ in F is left irreducible.
3. All the FDs in R can be constructed from the FDs in F by using Armstrong's Axioms.
4. No FD can be eliminated from F without losing the ability to construct the FDs in R as in 3.

The following algorithm – similar to one in reference [Ul] – will be shown in Theorem 5.3.6 to result in dependency preserving 3NF projections:

Algorithm 5.3.5 – The Dependency Preserving Decomposition Algorithm: Let F be a set of functional dependencies that is a minimal cover for a relation R. Then let the decomposition consist of all the projections Project(R, X ∪ A) where $X \rightarrow A$ is in F.

The following theorem – from [Ul] – ensures that the application of the foregoing algorithm will result in a dependency preserving decomposition into 3NF.

Theorem 5.3.6: The projections resulting from the Dependency Preserving Decomposition Algorithm form a dependency preserving decomposition into 3NF.

The following inference may allow us to simplify the algorithm by replacing many projections with one.

Inference 5.3.7: Let $X \rightarrow A_1, \ldots X \rightarrow A_n$ be functional dependencies in a minimal cover F for relation R. Then we can modify the Dependency Preserving Algorithm by replacing Project(R, X ∪ A_1), .. Project(R, X ∪ A_n) with Project[R, X ∪ $\{A_1, \ldots A_n\}$].

The next theorem – also from [Ul] – allows us to add a component to the result of the Dependency Preserving Decomposition Algorithm to ensure that the decomposition is also non loss.

Theorem 5.3.8: Let $\{R_1, \ldots R_n\}$ be the projections that form a decomposition of R resulting from the Dependency Preserving Decomposition Algorithm. Further, let C be a set of attributes that is a candidate key for R. Then $\{R_1, \ldots R_n, Project(R, C)\}$ is a non loss, dependency preserving decomposition into 3NF.

The following inference may make it unnecessary to add Project(R, C) to the decomposition.

Inference 5.3.9: Let R and $\{R_1, \ldots R_n\}$ be the projections that form a decomposition of R resulting from the Dependency Preserving Decomposition Algorithm. If the attributes of any R_i are a super key for R, then $\{R_1, \ldots R_n\}$ is a non loss, dependency preserving decomposition into 3NF.

It follows from the preceding theorem that every relation can be replaced by a non loss, dependency preserving decomposition into 3NF. Further, we know from Inference 4.3.4 that the components of the decomposition are independently updateable.

Example 2:
A Decomposition of the preceding Example 1 that Results in Independently Updateable Projections

Let's consider again the ServiceRequests relation from the preceding Example 1. From Theorem 5.3.8 we know that there exists a non loss, 3NF decomposition that, unlike the decomposition in Example 1, preserves dependencies.

ServiceRequests

ServNum	EqNum	CustID	CustReg	ServOrg
SN10	EQ08	CN09	CR35	Org50
SN12	EQ16	CN25	CR28	Org22
SN34	EQ05	CN09	CR35	Org71
SN26	EQ05	CN18	CR11	Org33
SN35	EQ16	CN25	CR28	Org22

First we list functional dependencies that form a minimal cover for ServiceRequests along with the corresponding projections for Algorithm 5.3.5:

ServNum → EqNum	Project(ServiceRequests, {ServNum, EqNum})
ServNum → CustID	Project(ServiceRequests, {ServNum, CustID})
CustID → CustReg	Project(ServiceRequests, {CustID, CustReg})
{EqNum, CustReg} → ServOrg	Project(ServiceRequests, {EqNum, CustReg, ServOrg})

By Inference 5.3.7, Project(ServiceRequests, {ServNum, EqNum}) and Project (ServiceRequests, {ServNum, CustID}) can be replaced by Project(ServiceRequests, {ServNum, EqNum, CustID}).

Also the candidate key ServNum appears in two of the projections so by Inference 5.3.9 it isn't necessary to add Project(ServiceRequests, ServNum) to our decomposition and thus the following is a non loss, dependency preserving, 3NF decomposition:

Project(ServiceRequests, {ServNum, EqNum, CustID})
Project(ServiceRequests, {CustID, CustReg})
Project(ServiceRequests, {EqNum, CustReg, ServOrg})

Also, from Inference 4.3.4, we know that this decomposition is independently updateable. Next, we'll use our sample data to examine a particular instance of the decomposition.

A

CustID	CustReg
CN09	CR35
CN25	CR28
CN18	CR11

B

EqNum	CustReg	ServOrg
EQ08	CR35	Org50
EQ16	CR28	Org22
EQ05	CR35	Org71
EQ05	CR11	Org33

C

ServNum	EqNum	CustID
SN10	EQ08	CN09
SN12	EQ16	CN25
SN34	EQ05	CN09
SN26	EQ05	CN18
SN35	EQ16	CN25

Consider what happens if Customer CN018 moves to region CR035. Relation A updated with this new value of CustReg is represented to the right. The result of taking the Join of the updated relation A on the right with relations B and C above is presented below.

CustID	CustReg
CN09	CR35
CN25	CR28
CN18	*CR35*

As expected, the independent updating of relation A – unlike Example 1 – doesn't lead to any problems in the join of the relations in the decomposition.

A Join B Join C

ServNum	EqNum	CustID	CustReg	ServOrg
SN10	EQ08	CN09	CR35	Org50
SN12	EQ16	CN25	CR28	Org22
SN34	EQ05	CN09	CR35	Org71
SN26	EQ05	CN18	CR35	Org71
SN35	EQ16	CN25	CR28	Org22

Section 5.4 Boyce/Codd Normal Form

The definition of Boyce/Codd normal form differs from that of 3NF only in that the dependent in the full functional dependency isn't restricted to be an informational attribute. However, unlike 3NF, there is no guarantee that we can always attain a decomposition into BCNF that is independently updateable.

Boyce/Codd Normal Form (BCNF): A relation is in BCNF if and only if every determinant of an attribute in a non trivial full functional dependency is a candidate key.

Inference 5.4.1: A relation in BCNF is also in 3NF.

The next two inferences present alternative, equivalent statements for the definition of BCNF:

Inference 5.4.2: A relation is in BCNF if and only if every determinant of an attribute in a non trivial functional dependency is a super key.

The following allows the dependent in the functional dependency to contain more than one attribute.

Inference 5.4.3: A relation is in BCNF if and only if every determinant in a non trivial functional dependency is a super key.

The following inference provides a criterion that assures that certain relations are in BCNF.

Inference 5.4.4: If a relation is in 3NF and has no overlapping candidate keys, then it's also in BCNF.

The inference below provides a condition for deciding that a relation isn't in BCNF.

Inference 5.4.5: A relation is not in BCNF if there is an attribute, A, that's fully functionally dependent on a set of attributes, X, that isn't a candidate key and A isn't an attribute in X.

Update Anomalies When a Relation is not in BCNF:

Insert: To add a non candidate key determinant value and the corresponding dependent attribute value a row with these values must be added. However, there may be no primary key value for which such a row would be valid and thus no way to record the fact that the dependent attribute value corresponds to this non candidate key value.

Delete: If the last row containing a specific value for a non candidate key determinant is deleted, the fact that the dependent attribute value on that row corresponds to the non candidate key value is lost. This correspondence may be significant apart from the appearance of these values on the deleted row.

Update: To update the value for an attribute that depends on a non candidate key, it would be necessary to update it in every row that the corresponding non candidate key value appears.

Normalization Procedure:

As for 2NF and one of the procedures for attaining 3NF, we'll continue to replace relations that are not in BCNF with non loss decompositions until all the relations that replace the original are in BCNF. Again Heath's Theorem provides the basis for the decompositions.

Starting with a relation that's not in BCNF, repeat steps 1 and 2 below until all the replacement relations from step 2 are in BCNF:

1) Let Y be the set of all the attributes that are each fully functionally dependent on a set of attributes, X, that isn't a candidate key and has no attributes in common with Y. Let Z be all the attributes that aren't in X or Y.

2) Replace the relation by the two relations formed by its projections on $X \cup Y$ and $X \cup Z$.

Since $X \rightarrow Y$, the projections on $X \cup Y$ and $X \cup Z$ satisfy the requirements of Heath's Theorem and hence form a non loss decomposition of the original relation.

Example 1: Normalizing a Relation to BCNF

Orders

For this relation, the order with ONum contains the product with ProdID and name ProdNam for Quantity units. The Product Names are unique for each Product ID. The candidate keys for this relation are {ONum, ProdID} and {ONum, ProdNam}. The informational attribute, Quantity, is only de-

ONum	ProdID	ProdNam	Quantity
ON16	P18	Rake	3
ON16	P21	Shovel	1
ON16	P14	Hoe	4
ON23	P09	Pick	6
ON23	P21	Shovel	1

pendent on the candidate keys and therefore the relation is in 3NF. However, we have ProdID → ProdNam and ProdNam → ProdID. Since there's a determinant, ProdID (and also ProdNam), that is not a candidate key, the relation is not in BCNF.

Here are the two BCNF relations produced by normalizing the Orders relation.

ProdID	ProdNam
P18	Rake
P21	Shovel
P14	Hoe
P09	Pick

ONum	ProdID	Quantity
ON16	P18	3
ON16	P21	1
ON16	P14	4
ON23	P09	6
ON23	P21	1

Example 2: A Normalization to BCNF that Results in Non Independently Updateable Relations

This example is similar to one in [Ri]. In relation Seminar an Attendee will attend a lecture with lecture number LecNum at time Hour on the day of the seminar. Assume that the name Attendee is unique and that each lecture is given only at one time. There are candidate keys {Attendee, Hour} and {Attendee, LecNum} and the full FD LecNum→Hour. The relation is in 3NF because there are no informational attributes; it's not in BCNF because LecNum→Hour.

Seminar

Attendee	Hour	LecNum
Wilson	10:30	L02
Lenox	14:00	L08
Jones	09:00	L04
Lenox	10:30	L01
Peterson	14:00	L08

The normalization procedure yields the BCNF projections to the right. Project1 has one candidate key {LecNum, Attendee}; Project2 has candidate key LecNum. Project1 has been updated by adding the italicized row. However, doing the join reveals a violation of an FD due to this update as shown below.

Project1

LecNum	Attendee
L02	Wilson
L08	Lenox
L04	Jones
L01	Lenox
L08	Peterson
L01	*Wilson*

Project2

LecNum	Hour
L02	10:30
L08	14:00
L04	09:00
L01	10:30

In the JOIN of the projections, we see that Wilson is scheduled for two lectures at the same time. This occurs because the FD {Attendee, Hour}→LecNum was not preserved in the decomposition and the projections cannot be updated independently. To update Project1 properly, one must first check the values of the rows in both projections to ensure that the new row is valid.

Seminar

Attendee	Hour	LecNum
Wilson	*10:30*	*L02*
Lenox	14:00	L08
Jones	09:00	L04
Lenox	10:30	L01
Peterson	14:00	L08
Wilson	*10:30*	*L01*

For this example, then, the BCNF normalization procedure results in non independently updateable projections.

Section 5.5 Fourth Normal Form

Fourth Normal Form is achieved by eliminating non trivial Multivalued Dependencies whose determinant isn't a super key; we'll see that the only non trivial MVDs that remain are just FDs. Clearly, it's best to avoid creating MVDs that violate 4NF by – as stated in Note 5.1.1 in Section 5.1 – not resolving more than one repeating group with a single relation.

Fourth Normal Form (4NF): A Relation, R, is in 4NF if and only if whenever there exists subsets X, Y of the attributes of R such that there is a non trivial MVD $X \twoheadrightarrow Y$, then X is a super key.

Inference 5.5.1: If R is a relation in 4NF, then every non-trivial MVD is a non-trivial FD whose determinant is a super key.

Inference 5.5.2: A relation in 4NF is also in BCNF and thus in all lower normal forms.

The following two conditions due to C. J. Date concerning the existence of simple (one attribute) candidate keys may make it possible to know that a relation is in 4NF without having to find the MVDs. Recall that a simple candidate key is comprised of only one attribute.

A condition for guaranteeing 4NF: If a relation is in BCNF and some candidate key is simple then the relation is in 4NF. [Da3]

Since a relation in 5NF is also in 4NF, the following is also relevant for 4NF.

A condition for guaranteeing 5NF: If a relation is in 3NF and every candidate key is simple then the relation is in 5NF. [Da3]

Update Anomalies When a Relation is not in 4NF:

If a relation is not in 4NF, then there is a non trivial MVD $X \twoheadrightarrow Y | Z$ such that X is not a super key. Hence, there may be many Z-values corresponding to a given X-value and thus a Y-value can be valid on every row with this X-value and each of the Z-values.

Insert: To add a Y-value for some X-value, we must add all the rows for which this Y-value is valid. Thus, we must add a row consisting of an X-value, Y-value, Z-value for every Z-value that is valid for this X-value.

Delete: To delete a Y-value for a given X-value one must delete all the rows in which this Y-value appears with this X-value.

Update: To update a Y-value for a given X-value one must update all the rows in which this Y-value appears with this X-value.

Normalization Procedure:

This procedure requires that one find all the MVDs in the relation to be normalized. We'll continue to replace relations that are not in 4NF with non-loss decompositions until all the relations that replace the original are in 4NF. Fagin's Theorem provides the basis for the decompositions.

Starting with a relation that's not in 4NF, repeat the following until all the replacement relations from 2) are in 4NF:

1) Let $X \twoheadrightarrow Y | Z$ be a nontrivial MVD where X is not a super key.

2) Replace the relation by the two relations formed by its projections on X ∪ Y and X ∪ Z.

Since MVD $X \twoheadrightarrow Y | Z$, the projections on X ∪ Y and X ∪ Z satisfy the requirements of Fagin's Theorem and hence form a non-loss decomposition of the original relation.

Example: Normalizing a Relation into 4NF

(This relation appeared in the example at the end of Section 5.1 as the result of ignoring Note 5.1.1 and forming one relation from a table with two repeating groups.)

For each employee with last name LName the relation to the right contains that person's job title, one of his/her child's names and a project the employee has worked on. (We assume each LName refers to only one employee). The only candidate key is {LName, Child, Project} and the only other super key is {LName, JobTitle, Child, Project}.

Since there is an FD LName→JobTitle, we deduce from Inference 4.2.3 that LName→→JobTitle. Since LName isn't a super key, we must eliminate this MVD.

Emp

LName	JobTitle	Child	Project
Wilson	Analyst	Wanda	P04
Wilson	Analyst	Wanda	P23
Wilson	Analyst	William	P04
Wilson	Analyst	William	P23
Wilson	Analyst	Wendy	P04
Wilson	Analyst	Wendy	P23
Mason	Programmer	Matthew	P23
Johnson	Engineer	James	P04
Johnson	Engineer	James	P15
Johnson	Engineer	James	P46
Johnson	Engineer	Janet	P04
Johnson	Engineer	Janet	P15
Johnson	Engineer	Janet	P46

Doing a step of the normalization procedure to remove LName→→JobTitle yields the relations to the right.

A

LName	JobTitle
Wilson	Analyst
Mason	Programmer
Johnson	Engineer

B

LName	Child	Project
Wilson	Wanda	P04
Wilson	Wanda	P23
Wilson	William	P04
Wilson	William	P23
Wilson	Wendy	P04
Wilson	Wendy	P23
Mason	Matthew	P23
Johnson	James	P04
Johnson	James	P15
Johnson	James	P46
Johnson	Janet	P04
Johnson	Janet	P15
Johnson	Janet	P46

Next, we consider the MVD LName→→Child in relation B.

Doing a step of the normalization procedure to remove LName→→Child yields the relations to the right.

Thus, relations A, C, and D form a 4NF decomposition of the original relation and the normalization procedure is complete.

C

LName	Child
Wilson	Wanda
Wilson	William
Wilson	Wendy
Mason	Matthew
Johnson	James
Johnson	Janet

D

LName	Project
Wilson	P04
Wilson	P23
Mason	P23
Johnson	P04
Johnson	P15
Johnson	P46

Section 5.6 Fifth Normal Form

Fifth Normal Form is closely related to the concept of join dependency. Since join dependencies are difficult to discern, it can be hard to confirm 5NF for a given relation. Similarly, though a normalization procedure to attain 5NF is presented, it may be very difficult to implement. Fortunately, relations that are in 4NF but not in 5NF are considered to be extremely unlikely to occur in real world situations; Fagin [Fa2] describes such relations as "bizarre." However, 5NF does provide a logical completion to the topic of normalizing relations using projection and join.

For expediency, we repeat the following definition from Section 4.4:

Join Dependency (JD): Let R be a relation and let $X_1, X_2 \ldots X_n$ be subsets of the attributes of R. Then R is said to satisfy the JD $*(X_1, X_2 \ldots X_n)$ if and only if R is equal to the join of its projections on $X_1, X_2 \ldots X_n$. Alternatively, R is said to satisfy the JD $*(X_1, X_2 \ldots X_n)$ if and only if the projections of R on $X_1, X_2 \ldots X_n$ form a non-loss decomposition of R.

Before defining Fifth Normal Form, it's necessary to discuss what it means for a JD to be "the result of candidate keys" or, as described by Fagin [Fa2], a JD that's a logical consequence of the set of candidate key dependencies in the relation. Fortunately, there's a conceptually straightforward algorithm to decide if a JD has this property that will serve as a pragmatic definition of it. That is, we'll say that a JD is the result of candidate keys if it satisfies the test provided by the algorithm. In the following, we present this algorithm – similar to one that appears in reference [Fa2] – that's used to determine whether a JD is the result of candidate keys.

Algorithm 5.6.1 To Determine if a JD is the Result of Candidate Keys: For a relation, R, and a $JD^*(X_1, X_2, \ldots X_n)$ perform the following steps to determine if the JD is "the result of candidate keys."

Step 1) Initialize a set, A, as $\{X_1, X_2, \ldots X_n\}$

Step 2) If there is a candidate key for R that's in two of the attribute sets in A, replace these two attribute sets in A by their set union – thereby decreasing the number of attribute sets in A by one.

Repeat Step 2 as long as there's some candidate key that's in two of the remaining attribute sets in A.

If – after performing the algorithm – there's an attribute set in A with all the attributes of R, we say that the algorithm "succeeds" for R and the $JD^*(X_1, X_2, \ldots X_n)$. Otherwise, we say that it "fails."

Finally, for a relation R, we say that a $JD^*(X_1, X_2, \ldots X_n)$ is "the result of candidate keys" if Algorithm 5.6.1 succeeds for R and the $JD^*(X_1, X_2, \ldots X_n)$.

We're now in a position to define Fifth Normal Form as follows:

Fifth Normal Form (5NF): A Relation, R, is in 5NF if every JD in R is the result of candidate keys. That is, Algorithm 5.6.1 succeeds for R and every JD in R.

Inference 5.6.2: A relation in 5NF is also in 4NF and thus in all lower normal forms.

The following condition, also mentioned in the last section, concerning the existence of simple (one attribute) candidate keys might make it possible to know that a relation is in 5NF without having to find the join dependencies in the relation.

A condition for guaranteeing 5NF: If a relation is in 3NF and every key is simple, then the relation is in 5NF. [Da3]

Example 1: A Join Dependency that's the Result of Candidate Keys

Each row of a relation R contains information about a company. The set of attributes is {I, N, S, P} where: I = unique company ID, Name = unique company name, S = State in which the company headquarters is located, P = Profits last year. The candidate keys are N and I; the following is a minimal cover for the functional dependencies: I→N, N→I, I→S, I→P

Define 3 subsets of the attributes as: IN={I, N}, IP={I, P} and NS={N, S}

First, we'll use Algorithm 4.4.1 to show that the projections of R on IN, IP, and NS form a non-loss decomposition of R.

The initial table for Algorithm 4.4.1 is on the right. Using the algorithm with I→N changes b_{22} to a_2. Similarly, N→I changes b_{31} to a_1; I→S changes both b_{13} and b_{23} to a_3. The table resulting from these changes is presented below.

	I	N	S	P
IN	a_1	a_2	b_{13}	b_{14}
IP	a_1	b_{22}	b_{23}	a_4
NS	b_{31}	a_2	a_3	b_{34}

Since the second row is $a_1 \ldots a_4$ we can terminate the algorithm. We deduce from Theorem 4.4.2 that the projections on the attribute sets IN, IP and NS form a non-loss decomposition and thus – by definition – R satisfies JD *(IN, IP, NS).

	I	N	S	P
IN	a_1	a_2	a_3	b_{14}
IP	a_1	a_2	a_3	a_4
NS	a_1	a_2	a_3	b_{34}

Next, we'll use Algorithm 5.6.1 to show that the JD *(IN, IP, NS) is the result of candidate keys:
Step 1) Initialize A ={IN, IP, NS}.
Step 2) For candidate key I, A becomes {INP, NS} where INP denotes {I, N, P}.
Repeat Step 2) For candidate key N, A becomes {INPS} where INPS denotes {I, N, P, S}.

Thus the algorithm succeeds and JD *(IN, IP, NS} is the result of candidate keys.

Example 2: A JD that isn't the Result of Candidate Keys

Each row of a relation R contains information about a course that will be offered in the coming semester. All the courses meet Monday through Friday. The set of attributes is {InstID, Name, Time, Loc, Dept, Course} where: InstID = an instructor ID, Name = instructor's last name, Time = time the course is offered, Loc = room/building, Dept = department, Course = the course name.

The candidate keys for R are: {InstID, Time} and (Loc, Time}. Let INLD={InstID, Name, Loc, Dept}, ITLC={InstID, Time, Loc, Course} and NTDC={Name, Time, Dept, Course}.

In a preceding example in Section 4.4, we showed that R is non-loss decomposable into the projections on INLD, ITLC and NTDC. Thus by definition R satisfies JD *(INLD, ITLC, NTDC}.

Using Algorithm 5.6.1 to find out if this JD is the "result of candidate keys":
Step 1) Initialize A={INLD, ITLC, NTDC}.
Step 2) For candidate key {InstID, Time}, A doesn't change.
Repeat Step 2) For candidate key {Loc, Time}, A doesn't change.

Thus the algorithm fails, JD *(INLD, ITLC, NTDC} isn't the result of candidate keys and R isn't in 5NF.

<u>Update Anomalies When a Relation is not in 5NF:</u>

As will be demonstrated in the examples that conclude this section, it's possible for a relation R not in 5NF to have a $JD^*(X_1, X_2, \ldots X_n)$ that holds only if certain constraints – specified in the definition of R – among the rows in R are satisfied. In particular, the existence of some row may require that some other row also be in R. If it's required that this JD remain valid, then any updates to R must conform to these constraints or the decomposition and join associated with a $JD^*(X_1, X_2, \ldots X_n)$ may not result in R. Hence, a relation that is not in 5NF can have implicit constraints among the rows causing update anomalies such as:

<u>Insert:</u> Adding a row for which the JD requires the presence of another row without also adding the required row could cause the JD to become invalid.

<u>Delete:</u> Deleting a row required by an existing row without also deleting the existing row could cause the JD to become invalid.

To show that the preceding update anomalies can't occur for a relation in 5NF, we first present the following two inferences that serve to characterize 5NF and also will be used to prove Inference 5.6.5.

Inference 5.6.3: Let R be a relation and let $X_1, X_2, \ldots X_m$ be subsets of the attributes of R whose union was formed in the process of applying Algorithm 5.6.1. Then $Project(R, X_1 \cup X_2 \ldots \cup X_m) = Project(R, X_1)$ JOIN $Project(R, X_2) \ldots$ JOIN $Project(R, X_m)$.

As mentioned above, some JDs only hold for a relation R when the values in the relation satisfy certain constraints that are specified in the definition of R. The following inference assures us that this restriction doesn't apply to JDs for which Algorithm 5.6.1 succeeds. The fact that the algorithm succeeds for a relation R and some subsets of its attributes $\{X_1, X_2, \ldots X_n\}$ is itself sufficient to ensure that the projections of R on $X_1, X_2, \ldots X_n$ form a non-loss decomposition of R.

Inference 5.6.4: Let R be a relation and $X_1, X_2, \ldots X_n$ be subsets of the attributes of R for which Algorithm 5.6.1.succeeds. Then the projections of R on $X_1, X_2, \ldots X_n$ form a non-loss decomposition of R.

The following inference proves that a relation in 5NF will not have the type of update anomalies described above for relations not in 5NF.

Inference 5.6.5: For a relation R in 5NF, the addition or deletion of a row will never cause the violation of a join dependency in R. That is, for any $JD^*(X_1, X_2, \ldots X_n)$, R will still be equal to the join of its projections on $X_1, X_2 \ldots X_n$ after a row is added to or deleted from R.

<u>Normalization Procedure:</u> Although a normalization procedure is described below, it can be difficult to carry out because it requires that one find Join Dependencies. As usual, we'll continue replacing relations that aren't in 5NF with non-loss decompositions until all the relations that replace the original are in 5NF.

Starting with a relation that's not in 5NF, repeat the following until all the replacement relations from 2) are in 5NF:

1) Let $JD^*(X_1, \ldots X_n)$ be a non-trivial join dependency such that Algorithm 5.6.1 fails.

2) Replace the relation by the relations formed by its projections on $X_1, \ldots X_n$.

By the definition of Join Dependency, these projections form a non-loss decomposition of R.

Example 1: A Relation that's in 4NF but not in 5NF

For this example, which appears in [Fa2], a relation R consists of the attributes A, P, and C where each row contains the name of a sales Agent, A, who represents a Product, P, for some Company, C.

Additionally, the acceptable values for the attributes are subject to the following unusual constraint: If Agent a represents Product p for Company c' and a' represents p for c and a represents p' for c, then a represents p for c. That is, if {a,p,c'}, {a',p,c} and {a,p',c} are rows in R, then {a,p,c} is also a row in R. This constraint is chosen to ensure that a non loss decomposition exists as shown below.

Proof that R with the specified constraint isn't in 5NF:

We'll prove that R satisfies the JD*({A,P},{P,C},{A,C}) that isn't the result of candidate keys.

If {a,p,c} is a row in Project(R,{A,P}) Join Project(R,{P,C}) Join Project(R,{A,C}), then by the general definition of join in Section 3.3, we know {a,p}, {p,c} and {a,c} are rows in Project(R,{A,P}), Project(R,{P,C}), and Project(R,{A,C}) respectively. Thus there must be values a', p', c' such that {a,p,c'}, {a',p,c} and {a,p',c} are rows in R. By the constraint it follows that {a,p,c} is a row in R.

Next, if {a,p,c} is a row in R, then {a,p}, {p,c} and {a,c} are rows in Project(R,{A,P}), Project(R,{P,C}), and Project(R,{A,C}) respectively. Thus {a,p,c} is a row in Project(R,{A,P}) Join Project(R,{P,C}) and also in Project(R,{A,P}) Join Project (R,{P,C}) Join Project(R,{A,C}).

Thus R=Project(R,{A,P}) Join Project(R,{P,C}) Join Project(R,{A,C}) so R has the JD*({A,P},{P,C},{A,C}). Next we'll show that this JD isn't the result of candidate keys.

The only candidate key for R is {A,P,C}. Thus using Algorithm 5.6.1 to find out if the JD *({A,P},{P,C},{A,C}) is the result of candidate keys we have:
Step 1) Initialize S={{A,P}, {P,C}, {A,C}}
Step 2) For the candidate key {A,P,C}, S doesn't change.

Since the algorithm fails, the JD*({A,P},{P,C},{A,C}) isn't the result of candidate keys and thus, by definition, R isn't in 5NF.

Proof that R with the specified constraint is in 4NF:

We've shown above that if the constraint holds then there's a JD*({A,P},{P,C},{A,C}).

We'll now prove that if there's a JD*({A,P},{P,C},{A,C}), then the constraint is satisfied: Let {a,p,c'}, {a',p,c} and {a,p',c} be rows in R. We must show that {a,p,c} is a row in R. {a,p}, {p,c} and {a,c} are rows in Project(R,{A,P}), Project(R,{P,C}), and Project(R,{A,C}) respectively. Hence, {a,p,c} is a row in Project(R,{A,P}) Join Project (R,{P,C}) Join Project (R,{A,C}) that equals R because, by assumption, the JD*({A,P},{P,C},{A,C}) holds. Thus the constraint is satisfied. We'll use this result in the following.

One can verify that R= Project(R,{A,P}) Join Project (R,{P,C}) Join Project(R,{A,C}) for the instance of R on the right and thus the JD*({A,P},{P,C},{A,C}) holds; hence, from the discussion immediately above, this instance of R satisfies the aforementioned constraint.

R		
A	P	C
Smith	Glassware	Apco
Jones	Cutlery	Beldin
Smith	Plates	Comax
Jones	Cookware	Dexler
Cory	Cutlery	Dexler
Jones	Cutlery	Dexler

If R isn't in 4NF, there must be a non-trivial MVD that isn't a super-key. We'll show that R is in 4NF because there are no non-trivial MVDs.

The only possible non trivial MVDs are:
A→→P|C, P→→ A|C and C→→A|P.

Considering A→→P|C first, we note that from the given data, Glassware and Comax each appear on a row with Smith, but Glassware, Comax and Smith don't appear on a row together. Hence, by Inference 4.2.1, A→→P|C isn't an MVD.

Similarly, one could demonstrate that the other possibilities also aren't MVDs and thus R is in 4NF.

Example 2: Update Anomalies for a Relation in 4NF but not in 5NF

To the right, we repeat the instance of a relation that was used in the previous example to show that R is in 4NF.

Also, the values in the relation are required to satisfy the constraint: If {a, p, c'}, {a', p, c} and {a, p', c} are rows in R, then {a, p, c} is also a row in R. We also showed in the previous example that this instance does, indeed, satisfy the constraint.

R

Agent	Product	Company
Smith	Glassware	Apco
Jones	Cutlery	Beldin
Smith	Plates	Comax
Jones	Cookware	Dexler
Cory	Cutlery	Dexler
Jones	Cutlery	Dexler

We'll cite two update anomalies for this instance of R:

1) We can't delete the row {Jones, Cutlery, Dexler} without also deleting one of the rows {Jones, Cutlery, Beldin}, {Jones, Cookware, Dexler} or {Cory, Cutlery, Dexler} because by the constraint these last three rows imply the presence of the first where {a , p, c, a', p', c'} equals in order {Jones ,Cutlery, Dexler, Cory, Cookware, Beldin}.

2) We couldn't add a row {Bond, Glassware, Comax} without also adding the row {Smith, Glassware, Comax} because {Bond, Glassware, Comax} along with the existing rows {Smith, Glassware, Apco} and {Smith, Plates, Comax} would require the presence of {Smith, Glassware, Comax} where {a, p, c, a', p', c'} equals in order {Smith, Glassware, Comax, Bond, Plates, Apco}.

Both of these update anomalies are avoided by replacing R with relations that are in 5NF. We'll demonstrate this for anomaly 2. Let AP=Project(R,{A,P}), PC=Project(R,{P,C}) and AC=Project(R,{A,C}).

Applying the 5NF normalization procedure with the JD*({A,P},{P,C},{A,C}), we replace R by AP, PC and AC. Thus R can be non-loss decomposed into the 5NF relations AP, PC and AC.

To the right is the decomposition of this instance of R. The italicized rows were added to show that anomaly 2 above doesn't occur when we update the decomposition. These rows in effect add the row {Bond,Glassware,Comax} to R.

AP

Agent	Product
Smith	Glassware
Jones	Cutlery
Smith	Plates
Jones	Cookware
Cory	Cutlery
Bond	*Glassware*

PC

Product	Company
Glassware	Apco
Cutlery	Beldin
Plates	Comax
Cookware	Dexler
Cutlery	Dexler
Glassware	*Comax*

AC

Agent	Company
Smith	Apco
Jones	Beldin
Smith	Comax
Jones	Dexler
Cory	Dexler
Bond	*Comax*

The relations on the right exhibit how the row {Bond,Glassware,Comax} along with the required {Smith,Glassware,Comax} was added to R.

Using the decomposition, instead of the original relation ensures that the constraint is always observed and thus avoids the need to be concerned about the update anomalies.

AP Join PC

Agent	Product	Company
Smith	Glassware	Apco
Smith	Glassware	Comax
Jones	Cutlery	Beldin
Jones	Cutlery	Dexler
Smith	Plates	Comax
Jones	Cookware	Dexler
Cory	Cutlery	Beldin
Cory	Cutlery	Dexler
Bond	Glassware	Apco
Bond	Glassware	Comax

(AP Join PC) Join AC

Agent	Product	Company
Smith	Glassware	Apco
Jones	Cutlery	Beldin
Smith	Plates	Comax
Jones	Cookware	Dexler
Cory	Cutlery	Dexler
Jones	Cutlery	Dexler
Smith	*Glassware*	*Comax*
Bond	*Glassware*	*Comax*

Appendix: Proofs

Proofs for Chapter 3 – Relational Algebra

Union Properties: UNION is both commutative and associative.

Recall from Chapter 3 that a row will appear in the UNION if and only if the row also appears in either of the original relations.

Proof of Commutivity: A row in A UNION B must be in A or in B and, therefore, also in B UNION A. Similarly, any row in B UNION A is also in A UNION B. Thus, UNION is commutative.

Proof of Associativity: A row in A UNION (B UNION C) must be in A or in (B UNION C) which implies that the row is in A or in B or in C. Hence, the row is in (A UNION B) UNION C. Likewise, a row in (A UNION B) UNION C is also in A UNION (B UNION C). Hence, UNION is associative.

Difference Properties: MINUS is not commutative and not associative. It's not distributive over UNION in the usual left to right sense, but is distributive "from the right." That is:

R MINUS (S UNION T) doesn't always = (R MINUS S) UNION (R MINUS T)
However, (R UNION S) MINUS T = (R MINUS T) UNION (S MINUS T)

Proofs that MINUS is not commutative, not associative and not distributive over UNION: This will be demonstrated by example. Let Relations R, S, and T each with one attribute - R_1 - have values as below:

Relation R	Relation S	Relation T	R MINUS S	S MINUS R
R_1	R_1	R_1	R_1	R_1
1	2	1	1	3
2	3	2		

Since R MINUS S ≠ S MINUS R, MINUS is not commutative.
Also, we have:

R MINUS (S MINUS T)	(R MINUS S) MINUS T
R_1	R_1
1	
2	

Since R MINUS (S MINUS T) ≠ (R MINUS S) MINUS T, MINUS is not associative.
Finally, consider the following:

R MINUS (S UNION T)	(R MINUS S) UNION (R MINUS T)
R_1	R_1
	1

Since R MINUS (S UNION T) ≠ (R MINUS S) UNION (R MINUS T), MINUS is not distributive over UNION in the usual "left to right" sense.

Proof that Difference is distributive 'from the right' over UNION:

Let R, S and T be UNION compatible relations all with attributes $R_1, R_2, \ldots R_n$.

Let $r_1, r_2, \ldots r_n$ be a row in (R UNION S) MINUS T. Then it's a row in R or S and not a row in T. Thus it's a row in R MINUS T or in S MINUS T and, therefore, a row in (R MINUS T) UNION (S MINUS T).

Let $r_1, r_2, \ldots r_n$ be a row in (R MINUS T) UNION (S MINUS T). Then it's 'a row in R and not a row in T' or 'a row in S and not a row in T.' Hence it's a row in R or S and not a row in T and thus, a row in (R UNION S) MINUS T

Therefore, (R UNION S) MINUS T = (R MINUS T) UNION (S MINUS T) and difference is distributive over UNION "from the right."

Intersect Properties: INTERSECT is commutative, associative, and distributive over UNION.

A row will appear in the result relation if and only if the row appears in each of the original relations.

Proof of Commutivity: A row in R INTERSECT S must be in R and in S and, therefore, also in S INTERSECT R. Similarly, any row in S INTERSECT R is also in R INTERSECT S. Thus, INTERSECT is commutative.

Proof of Associativity: A row in R INTERSECT (S INTERSECT T) must be in R and in (S INTERSECT T) which implies that the row is in R and in S and in T. Hence, the row is in (R INTERSECT S) INTERSECT T. Likewise, a row in (R INTERSECT S) INTERSECT T is also in R INTERSECT (S INTERSECT T). Hence, INTERSECT is associative.

Proof of Distributivity over UNION: A row in R INTERSECT (S UNION T) is in R and in either S or in T (or both) If the row is in S, then it's in R Intersect S; If it's in T, then its in R Intersect T. Thus the row is in (R INTERSECT S) UNION (R INTERSECT T). Likewise, a row in (R INTERSECT S) UNION (R INTERSECT T) is either in R INTERSECT S or in R INTERSECT T and therefore in R and either S or T. Hence, the row is in R INTERSECT (S UNION T). Thus, INTERSECT is distributive over UNION.

Product Properties: TIMES is both commutative and associative and is distributive over UNION.

Thus, if R, S, and T are relations with no common attribute names, then we have:

Commutivity: R TIMES S = S TIMES R.
Associativity: R TIMES (S TIMES T) = (R TIMES S) TIMES T.

If R and S are relations with no common attributes where S and T are UNION compatible, then we have:

Distributivity over UNION: R TIMES (S UNION T) = (R TIMES S) UNION (R TIMES T)

Recall from Chapter 3 that for relations R with attribute names $R_1, \ldots R_m$ and S with attribute names $S_1, \ldots S_n$ the attribute values $r_1, \ldots r_m, s_1, \ldots s_n$ form a row in the PRODUCT if and only if:

1) $r_1, \ldots r_m$ form a row in R with each r_i in the column for R_i.

AND 2) $s_1, \ldots s_n$ form a row in S with each s_i in the column for S_i.

Proof of Commutivity: Let $r_1, \ldots r_m, s_1, \ldots s_n$ form a row in R TIMES S with each r_i and s_i in the column for R_i and S_i respectively. Then, since the order of attributes doesn't matter, $r_1, \ldots r_m, s_1, \ldots s_n$ also form a row in S TIMES R. Similarly, any row in S TIMES R is also in R TIMES S. Hence, TIMES is commutative.

Proof of Associativity: Let R , S and T be relations with attribute names $R_1, \ldots R_m, S_1, \ldots S_n$, and $T_1, \ldots T_k$. A row – $r_1, \ldots r_m, s_1, \ldots s_n, t_1, \ldots t_k$ – in R TIMES (S TIMES T) is also a row in (R TIMES S) TIMES T. Similarly, a row in (R TIMES S) TIMES T is also in R TIMES (S TIMES T). Thus, TIMES is associative.

Proof of Distributivity over UNION: R TIMES (S UNION T) = (R TIMES S) UNION (R TIMES T).

Let R and S be relations with attribute names $R_1, \ldots R_m, S_1, \ldots S_n$ and let T be a relation with attribute names $S_1, \ldots S_n$ so that S and T are UNION compatible.

Let $r_1, \ldots r_m, s_1, \ldots s_n$ be a row in R TIMES (S UNION T). Then:

1) $r_1, \ldots r_m$ form a row in R with each r_i in the column for R_i.
AND 2) $s_1, \ldots s_n$ form a row in S UNION T with each s_i in the column for S_i.

However, 2) holds if and only if $s_1, \ldots s_n$ form a row in S or in T. Thus 1) and 2) are equivalent to:

3) $r_1, \ldots r_m$ form a row in R AND 4) $s_1, \ldots s_n$ form a row in S.
OR
5) $r_1, \ldots r_m$ form a row in R AND 6) $s_1, \ldots s_n$ form a row in T.

But (3 AND 4) OR (5 AND 6) are precisely the conditions for $r_1, \ldots r_m, s_1, \ldots s_n$ to be a row in (R TIMES S) UNION (R TIMES T). Hence, R TIMES (S UNION T) = (R TIMES S) UNION (R TIMES T) and therefore TIMES is distributive over UNION.

– Proofs for Section 3.2: Intersect and Section 3.3: Product –

θ-Join Properties: θ-Join is commutative and also distributive over UNION. Expressions of the form R θ-Join($C_{R,S}$) (S θ-Join($D_{S,T}$) T) and (R θ-Join($C_{R,S}$) S) θ-Join($D_{S,T}$) T are associative.

Let the attribute names of relation R be $R_1, \ldots R_m$ with a row of attribute values denoted by $\{r_1, \ldots r_m\}$; let S be a relation with attribute names $S_1, \ldots S_n$ and attribute values denoted by $\{s_1, \ldots s_n\}$; let $C_{R,S}$ denote a comparison condition on the attributes of R and S. Then, from the discussion of θ-Join in Chapter 3, the attribute values $r_1, \ldots r_m, s_1, \ldots s_n$ form a row in R θ-Join($C_{R,S}$) S if and only if:

1) $r_1, \ldots r_m, s_1, \ldots s_n$ is a row in R TIMES S.
AND 2) The comparison expression evaluates to TRUE for the values $\{r_1, \ldots r_m\}$ and $\{s_1, \ldots s_n\}$.

<u>Proof of Commutivity of θ-Join:</u> Let $r_1, \ldots r_m, s_1, \ldots sn$ be a row in R θ-Join($C_{R,S}$) S. Then, by 1) it's also a row in R TIMES S. Since TIMES is commutative, $r_1, \ldots r_m, s_1, \ldots sn$ is also a row in S TIMES R. Also, the comparison operator is unchanged and, thus, TRUE for S TIMES R. Hence, $r_1, \ldots r_m, s_1, \ldots s_n$ is also a row in S θ-Join(C) R. Similarly, any row in S θ-Join($C_{R,S}$) R is also in S θ-Join($C_{R,S}$) R. Thus θ-Join is commutative.

Let R and S be as above and let T be a relation with attribute names $T_1, T_2 \ldots T_k$ with a row of attribute values denoted by $\{t_1, \ldots t_k\}$; let $D_{S,T}$ denote a condition on the attribute values of S and T.

<u>Proof of Associativity θ-Join:</u> The proof will use the necessary and sufficient conditions discussed above for a row to be in a θ-Join. Namely, 1) The row must be in the product of the input relations; 2) the attribute values in the row must satisfy the comparison condition.

To prove that R θ-Join($C_{R,S}$) (S θ-Join($D_{S,T}$) T) = (R θ-Join($C_{R,S}$) S) θ-Join($D_{S,T}$) T, we'll first show that any row in the left expression is also a row in the expression on the right.

Step 0. Let $r_1, \ldots r_m, s_1, \ldots s_n, t_1, \ldots t_k$ be a row in R θ-Join($C_{R,S}$) (S θ-Join($D_{S,T}$) T) where $\{r_1, \ldots r_m\}$, $\{s_1, \ldots s_n\}$, and $\{t_1, \ldots t_k\}$ are values for the attributes in R, S, and T respectively.

We'll show that it's also a row in (R θ-Join($C_{R,S}$) S) θ-Join($D_{S,T}$).

Step 1. $r_1, \ldots r_m, s_1, \ldots s_n, t_1, \ldots t_k$ is a row in (R TIMES S) TIMES T.
Because by Step 0 and the definition of θ-Join $r_1, \ldots r_m, s_1, \ldots s_n, t_1, \ldots t_k$ is a row in R TIMES (S TIMES T) which equals (R TIMES S) TIMES T.

Step 2. $r_1, \ldots r_m, s_1, \ldots s_n$ is a row in R TIMES S (From Step 1).

Step 3. $C_{R,S}$ evaluates to TRUE for $\{r_1, \ldots r_m\}$ and $\{s_1, \ldots s_n\}$.
From Step 0 we know that $C_{R,S}$ evaluates to TRUE for the values $\{r_1, \ldots r_m\}$ and $\{s_1, \ldots s_n, t_1, \ldots t_k\}$. However, since the t values are not used, $C_{R,S}$ evaluates to TRUE for $\{r_1, \ldots r_m\}$ and $\{s_1, \ldots s_n\}$.

Step 4. $r_1, \ldots r_m, s_1, \ldots s_n$ is a row in (R θ-Join($C_{R,S}$) S).
From Steps 2 and 3, the conditions for being a row in R θ-Join($C_{R,S}$) S are satisfied.

Step 5. $r_1, \ldots r_m, s_1, \ldots s_n, t_1, \ldots t_k$ is a row in (R θ-Join($C_{R,S}$) S) TIMES T. This follows from Steps 4 and 1.

Step 6. $\{r_1, \ldots r_m, s_1, \ldots s_n\}$, $\{t_1, \ldots t_k\}$ evaluates to TRUE for condition $D_{S,T}$.
From Step 0, $s_1, \ldots s_n, t_1, \ldots t_k$ is a row in S θ-Join($D_{S,T}$) T and thus $\{s_1, ..s_n\}$, $\{t_1, ..t_k\}$ satisfy condition $D_{S,T}$. Since the r values are not used, it follows that $\{r_1, \ldots r_m, s_1, \ldots s_n\}$, $\{t_1, \ldots t_k\}$ also satisfy condition $D_{S,T}$.

Step 7. $r_1, \ldots r_m, s_1, \ldots s_n, t_1, \ldots t_k$ is a row in (R θ-Join($C_{R,S}$) S) θ-Join($D_{S,T}$) T.
From Steps 5 and 6, the conditions for being a row in (R θ-Join($C_{R,S}$) S) θ-Join($D_{S,T}$) T are satisfied.

Hence, any row in R θ-Join($C_{R,S}$) (S θ-Join($D_{S,T}$) T) is also in (R θ-Join($C_{R,S}$) S) θ-Join($D_{S,T}$) T.

In the same way, we'll now show that any row in (R θ-Join($C_{R,S}$) S) θ-Join($D_{S,T}$) T is also a row in R θ-Join($C_{R,S}$) (S θ-Join($D_{S,T}$) T).

Step 0. Let $r_1, \ldots r_m, s_1, \ldots s_n, t_1, \ldots t_k$ be a row in (R θ-Join($C_{R,S}$) S) θ-Join($D_{S,T}$) T where $\{r_1, \ldots r_m\}$, $\{s_1, \ldots s_n\}$, and $\{t_1, \ldots t_k\}$ are values for the attributes in R, S, and T respectively.

We'll show that it's also a row in R θ-Join($C_{R,S}$) (S θ-Join($D_{S,T}$) T).

Step 1. $r_1, \ldots r_m, s_1, \ldots s_n, t_1, \ldots t_k$ is a row in R TIMES (S TIMES T).
Because by Step 0 and the definition of θ-Join $r_1, \ldots r_m, s_1, \ldots s_n, t_1, \ldots t_k$ is a row in (R TIMES S) TIMES T. Since TIMES is associative this equals R TIMES (S TIMES T).

Step 2. $s_1, \ldots s_n, t_1, \ldots t_k$ is a row in S TIMES T. (From Step 1).

Step 3. $D_{S,T}$ evaluates to TRUE for $\{ s_1, \ldots s_n \}$ and $\{t_1, \ldots t_k\}$.
From Step 0 we know that $D_{S,T}$ evaluates to TRUE for the values $\{r_1, \ldots r_m, s_1, \ldots s_n\}$ and $\{t_1, \ldots t_k\}$. However, since the r values are not used, $D_{S,T}$ evaluates to TRUE for $\{ s_1, \ldots s_n \}$ and $\{t_1, \ldots t_k\}$.

Step 4. $s_1, \ldots s_n, t_1, \ldots t_k$ form a row in (S θ-Join($D_{S,T}$) T).
From Steps 2 and 3, the conditions for being a row in S θ-Join($D_{S,T}$) T are satisfied.

Step 5. $r_1, \ldots r_m, s_1, \ldots s_n, t_1, \ldots t_k$ is a row in R TIMES (S θ-Join($D_{S,T}$) T). This follows from Steps 4 and 1.

Step 6. $\{r_1, \ldots r_m\}, \{s_1, \ldots s_n, t_1, \ldots t_k \}$ evaluates to TRUE for condition $C_{R,S}$.
From Step 0, $r_1, \ldots r_m, s_1, ..s_n$ is a row in R θ-Join($C_{R,S}$) S and thus $\{r_1, \ldots r_m\}$, $\{s_1, ..s_n\}$ satisfy condition $C_{R,S}$. Since the t values are not used, it follows that $\{r_1, \ldots r_m\}$, $\{s_1, \ldots s_n, t_1, \ldots t_k \}$ also satisfy condition $C_{R,S}$.

Step 7. $r_1, \ldots r_m, s_1, \ldots s_n, t_1, \ldots t_k$ is a row in R θ-Join($C_{R,S}$) (S θ-Join($D_{S,T}$) T).
From Steps 5 and 6, the conditions for being a row in R θ-Join($C_{R,S}$) (S θ-Join($D_{S,T}$) T) are satisfied.

Hence, any row in (R θ-Join($C_{R,S}$) S) θ-Join($D_{S,T}$) T) is also a row in R θ-Join($C_{R,S}$) (S θ-Join($D_{S,T}$) T.

We've now shown that R θ-Join($C_{R,S}$) (S θ-Join($D_{S,T}$) T) = (R θ-Join($C_{R,S}$) S) θ-Join($D_{S,T}$) T and thereby proved that expressions of this type are associative.

<u>Proof of Distributivity of θ-Join over UNION:</u> R θ-Join($C_{R,S}$) (S UNION T) = (R θ-Join($C_{R,S}$) S) UNION (R θ-Join($C_{R,S}$) T).

Let R and S be relations with attribute names $R_1, \ldots R_m$, and $S_1, \ldots S_n$ respectively and T be a relation that is UNION compatible with S with attribute values also denoted by $S_1, \ldots S_n$. Let $C_{R,S}$ be a comparison condition between R and S and, therefore, also between R and T.

Let $r_1, \ldots r_m, s_1, \ldots s_n$ be a row in R θ-Join($C_{R,S}$) (S UNION T).
Then:
1. $r_1, \ldots r_m, s_1, \ldots s_n$ is a row in R TIMES (S UNION T).
AND 2. The comparison expression evaluates to TRUE for the values $\{r_1, \ldots r_m\}$ and $\{s_1, \ldots s_n \}$ where $\{s_1, \ldots s_n \}$ is a row in (S UNION T).
This is equivalent to:
3. [($r_1, \ldots r_m, s_1, \ldots s_n$ is a row in R TIMES S) AND (The comparison expression evaluates to TRUE for the values $\{r_1, \ldots r_m\}$ and $\{s_1, \ldots s_n \}$ where $\{s_1, \ldots s_n \}$ is a row in S)].
OR 4. [($r_1, \ldots r_m, s_1, \ldots s_n$ is a row in R TIMES T) AND (The comparison expression evaluates to TRUE for the values $\{r_1, \ldots r_m\}$ and $\{s_1, \ldots s_n \}$ where $\{s_1, \ldots s_n \}$ is a row in T)].

Since 3 and 4 are the conditions for $r_1, \ldots r_m, s_1, \ldots s_n$ to be a row in (R θ-Join($C_{R,S}$) S) UNION (R θ-Join($C_{R,S}$) T), θ-Join is distributive over UNION.

Equi-Join Properties: Equi-Join is commutative and also distributive over UNION. Expressions of the form R Equi-Join($C_{R,S}$) (S Equi-Join($D_{S,T}$) T) and (R Equi-Join($C_{R,S}$) S) Equi-Join($D_{S,T}$) T are associative.

These properties have been proven for θ-Join and thus hold for the special case of the Equi-Join.

Natural Join

From Chapter 3, we have the following "binary" definition of Join:

Binary Definition of Join: Let R be a relation with attribute names $R_1, \ldots R_m, C_1, \ldots C_k$ and S a relation with attribute names $S_1, \ldots S_n, C_1, \ldots C_k$. The common attributes of R and S are $C_1, \ldots C_k$ and the heading of the result relation of the natural join of R and S is $R_1, \ldots R_m, S_1, \ldots S_n, C_1, \ldots C_k$. Then the attribute values $r_1, \ldots r_m, s_1, \ldots s_n, c_1, \ldots c_k$ form a row in the result relation if and only if:

1) $r_1, \ldots r_m, c_1, \ldots c_k$ form a row in R AND 2) $s_1, \ldots s_n, c_1, \ldots c_k$ form a row in S.

Natural Join Properties: Join is commutative, associative and distributive over UNION.

<u>Proof of Commutivity of Join</u>: R Join S = S Join R.
Let R and S be relations with $r_1, \ldots r_n, s_1, \ldots s_k, c_1, \ldots c_m$ forming a row in R Join S. The conditions for being a row in R Join S are the same as for S Join R. Hence, R Join S = S Join R and Join is commutative.

<u>Proof of Associativity of Join</u>: R Join (S Join T) = (R Join S) Join T.

We'll prove that Join is associative by using only the binary definition of Join.

First, we'll show that R Join (S Join T) and (R Join S) Join T have the same header:
The header for R Join (S Join T) consists of all the attribute names that appear in at least one of R or (S Join T). The header of S Join T is all the attributes that appear in at least one of S or T and thus the header of R Join (S Join T) consists of all the attribute names that appear in at least one of R, S, or T. Similarly, we can show that the header of (R Join S) Join T consists of these same attributes and thus R Join (S Join T) and (R Join S) Join T have the same header, namely, all the attribute names that appear in at least one of R, S, or T.

Next let R', S', and T' be the sets of attribute values in a row of R Join (S Join T) corresponding to R, S and T respectively. We'll show that the set union of these values also forms a row in (R Join S) Join T. Note that R', S', and T' include the values for any common attributes and thus may overlap.

1) The values in R' form a row in R.
Since R'U(S'UT') is a row in R Join (S Join T), it follows from the binary definition of join that the values (non common and common with (S Join T)) in R' form a row in R.
2) The values in (S'UT') form a row in (S Join T).
Since R'U (S'UT') is a row in R Join (S Join T), it follows from the binary definition of join that the values (non common and common with R) in (S'UT') form a row in (S Join T).
3) The values in S' form a row in S and the values in T' form a row in T.
This follows from 2 and the binary definition of Join.
4) The set union of the values in R' and S' forms a row in (R Join S).
This follows from 1 and 3 and the binary definition of Join.
5) The set union of the values in R', S' and T' forms a row in (R Join S) Join T.
This follows from 3 and 4 and the binary definition of Join.

Similarly, let R', S' and T' be the sets of attribute values in a row of (R Join S) Join T corresponding to R, S and T respectively. We'll show that these values also form a row in R Join (S Join T).
1) The values in T' form a row in T.
Since (R'US')UT' is a row in (R Join S) Join T, it follows from the binary definition of join that the values (non common and common with (R Join S)) in T' form a row in T.
2) The set union of the values in R' and S' forms a row in (R Join S).
Since R'U (S'UT') is a row in (R Join S) Join T, it follows from the binary definition of join that the values (non common and common with T) in (R'US') form a row in (R Join S).
3) The values in R' form a row in R and the values in S' form a row in S.
This follows from 2 and the binary definition of Join.
4) The set union of the values in S' and T' forms a row in (S Join T).
This follows from 1 and 3 and the binary definition of Join.
5) The values in R', S' and T' form a row in R Join (S Join T).
This follows from 3 and 4 and the binary definition of Join.

Thus R Join (S Join T) = (R Join S) Join T and Join is associative.

Proof of Distributivity of Join over UNION:

Let R be a relation with attribute names $R_1, \ldots R_n, C_1, \ldots C_m$ and S a relation with attribute names $S_1, \ldots S_k$, $C_1, \ldots C_m$. The common attributes of R and S are $C_1, \ldots C_m$. Further, let T have attribute names $S_1, \ldots S_k, C_1$, $\ldots C_m$. such that S and T are UNION compatible.

To show: R Join (S UNION T) = (R Join S) Union (R JOIN T).

Let $r_1, \ldots r_n, s_1, \ldots s_k, c_1, \ldots c$ form a row in R Join (S UNION T). Then:

1. $r_1, \ldots r_n, c_1, \ldots c_m$ form a row in R with each r_i in the column for R_i and c_i in the column for C_i.
AND
(2. $s_1, \ldots s_k, c_1, \ldots c_m$ form a row in S with each s_i in the column for S_i and c_i in the column for C_i.
OR
3. $s_1, \ldots s_k, c_1, \ldots c_m$ form a row in T with each s_i in the column for S_i and c_i in the column for C_i.)
Note that the above denotes 1. AND (2. OR 3.)

Let $r_1, \ldots r_n, s_1, \ldots s_k, c_1, \ldots c$ form a row in (R Join S) UNION (R JOIN T). Then:

(1. $r_1, \ldots r_n, c_1, \ldots c_m$ form a row in R with each r_i in the column for R_i and c_i in the column for Ci.
AND
2. $s_1, \ldots s_k, c_1, \ldots c_m$ form a row in S with each s_i in the column for S_i and c_i in the column for C_i.)
OR
(1. $r_1, \ldots r_n, c_1, \ldots c_m$ form a row in R with each r_i in the column for R_i and c_i in the column for Ci.
AND
3. $s_1, \ldots s_k, c_1, \ldots c_m$ form a row in T with each s_i in the column for S_i and c_i in the column for C_i.)
Note that the above denotes (1. AND 2.) OR (1. AND 3.).

However, the criteria 1. AND (2. OR 3.) is logically equivalent to (1. AND 2.) OR (1. AND 3.). Therefore, R Join (S UNION T) = (R Join S) Union (R JOIN T) and Join is distributive over UNION.

Inference 3.3.1: The natural join of two relations with no common attributes is equivalent to their Product.

Proof of Inference 3.3.1:

The requirement for Product that the relations have no common attribute names is met by assumption. Further, let $r_1, \ldots r_n$ be values for a relation R and $s_1, \ldots s_k$ values for a relation S. If there are no common attributes in R and S, then the conditions for $r_1, \ldots r_n, s_1, \ldots s_k$ to be a row in the natural join becomes:
1) $r_1, \ldots r_n$ form a row in R . AND 2) $s_1, \ldots s_k$ form a row in S.
These are precisely the conditions for a row being in the product thus proving Inference 3.3.1.

This completes the proof of Inference 3.3.1.

We repeat the two definitions of Join for use in the proof of Inference 3.3.2:

Binary Definition of Join: Let R be a relation with attribute names $R_1, \ldots R_m, C_1, \ldots C_k$ and S a relation with attribute names $S_1, \ldots S_n, C_1, \ldots C_k$. The common attributes of R and S are $C_1, \ldots C_k$ and the heading of the result relation of the natural join of R and S is $R_1, \ldots R_m, S_1, \ldots S_n, C_1, \ldots C_k$. Then, the attribute values $r_1, \ldots r_m, s_1, \ldots s_n, c_1, \ldots c_k$ form a row in the result relation if and only if:

1) $r_1, \ldots r_m, c_1, \ldots c_n$ form a row, in R. AND 2) $s_1, \ldots s_n, c_1, \ldots c_k$ form a row in S.

General Definition of Join: Let $R_1, R_2, \ldots R_n$ be a collection of relations. Then the result of the Natural Join of these relations has a heading with all the attribute names $A_1, A_2, \ldots A_m$ such that every A_i appears in at least one of $R_1, R_2, \ldots R_n$ and consists of all the rows $(a_1, a_2, \ldots a_m)$ where:

The values in $(a_1, a_2, \ldots a_m)$ corresponding to the attributes of R_i form a row in R_i for all $1 \leq i \leq n$.

Inference 3.3.2: The General Definition of Join is equivalent to the binary definition.

Proof of Inference 3.3.2:

We'll use the method of mathematical induction to show that the definitions yield the same result regardless of the number of relations involved.

First we'll show that the definitions are equivalent for two relations:

The Binary Definition requires that the heading consist of all the distinct attribute names in both relations. This implies that each attribute appears in at least one of the relations as stated in the General Definition. Conversely, if the heading consists of all the attributes that each appear in at least one of the relations, then the heading must consist of all the attributes in both relations; duplicates are ruled out because the values corresponding to the attributes of any relation must be a row in that relation. Thus the heading specifications are equivalent and since the conditions for what forms a row in the result are the same, the two definitions are equivalent.

Next we'll show that if the definitions are equivalent for n-1 relations, they must be equivalent for n.

Assume the definitions are equivalent for n-1 relations and let $R_1, R_2, \ldots R_n$ be a collection of relations. Since Join (by the binary definition) is commutative and associative, we can express the Join of $R_1, R_2, \ldots R_n$ as R_1 Join $(R_2 \ldots$ Join $R_n)$. By the assumption for n-1 relations, $R_2 \ldots$ Join R_n is the same for both definitions of Join. We've shown above that for two relations such as R_1 and $(R_2 \ldots$ Join $R_n)$, R_1 Join $(R_2 \ldots$ Join $R_n)$ is the same for both definitions. Thus R_1 Join $R_2 \ldots$ Join R_n is the same for either definition of Join.

Thus – by mathematical induction – the two definitions of Join are equivalent.

This completes the proof of Inference 3.3.2.

Left Outer θ-Join Properties: Left Outer θ-Join is not commutative or distributive over UNION. Expressions of the form Left Outer R θ-Join($C_{R,S}$) (S Left Outer θ-Join($D_{S,T}$) T) and (R Left Outer θ-Join($C_{R,S}$) S) Left Outer θ-Join($D_{S,T}$) T are associative.

Let the attribute names of relation R be $R_1, \ldots R_m$ with a row of attribute values denoted by $\{r_1, \ldots r_m\}$; let S be a relation with different attribute names $S_1, \ldots S_n$ and attribute values denoted by $\{s_1, \ldots s_n\}$; let $C_{R,S}$ denote a comparison condition on the attributes of R and S. Then, from the discussion of left outer θ-Join in Chapter 3, the attribute values $r_1, \ldots r_m, s_1, \ldots s_n$ form a row in the result relation if and only if:

Either 1) $r_1, \ldots r_m, s_1, \ldots s_n$ form a row in (R θ-Join($C_{R,S}$) S) with each r_i in the column for R_i and each s_i in the column for S_i.
Or 2) The values $r_1, \ldots r_m$ form a row in R with each r_i in the column for R_i, but do not appear together in any row of the corresponding θ-Join and $s_1, \ldots s_n$ are all null.

<u>Proof of non Commutivity of Left Outer θ-Join:</u> This will be shown by example. Let Relations R and S each with one attribute – R_1 and S_1 respectively – have values as below. Further, let $C_{R,S}$ be the comparison expression: $R_1 = S_1$.

Relation R   Relation S   R LEFT OUTER θ-JOIN($C_{R,S}$) S   S LEFT OUTER θ-JOIN($C_{R,S}$) R

R_1
1
2

S_1
1
3

R_1	S_1
1	1
2	Null

S_1	R_1
1	1
3	Null

Since R LEFT OUTER θ-JOIN($C_{R,S}$) S ≠ S LEFT OUTER θ-JOIN($C_{R,S}$) R, LEFT OUTER θ-JOIN is not commutative.

<u>Proof of Associativity of Left Outer θ-Join:</u>

Let R, S and T be relations with a row of attribute values denoted by $\{r_1, \ldots r_m\}$, $\{s_1, \ldots s_n\}$ and $\{t_1, \ldots t_k\}$ respectively. Let $C_{R,S}$ denote a comparison on the attributes of R and S; let $D_{S,T}$ denote a comparison on the attribute values of S and T. The proof will use the necessary and sufficient criteria discussed above for a row to be in a Left Outer θ-Join. Namely,
Criterion 1) The row is in the corresponding θ-JOIN of the input relations.
OR **Criterion 2)** The attribute values of the left relation must form a row in that relation, but don't appear together in a row in the corresponding θ-Join and the attribute values of the right relation are all null.

To prove that R Left Outer θ-Join($C_{R,S}$) (S Left Outer θ-Join($D_{S,T}$) T) = (R Left Outer θ-Join($C_{R,S}$) S) Left Outer θ-Join($D_{S,T}$) T, we'll first show that any row in the left expression is also a row in the right one.

We'll break the proof up into four cases depending upon whether the attribute values $s_1, \ldots s_n$ and $t_1, \ldots t_k$ are all Null or not for the values in the row $r_1, \ldots r_m, s_1, \ldots s_n, t_1, \ldots t_k$. The occurrence of all Nulls in $s_1, \ldots s_n$ or $t_1, \ldots t_k$ indicates that they were set to Null because the comparison expression was not TRUE for a row from the left relation for any row in the right relation in a Left Outer Join. Note that it's not possible for $r_1, \ldots r_m$ to be all Null since R is never the relation on the right.

Case 1) $s_1, \ldots s_n$ aren't all Null; $t_1, \ldots t_k$ aren't all Null.
Let $r_1, \ldots r_m, s_1, \ldots s_n, t_1, \ldots t_k$ be a row in R Left Outer θ-Join($C_{R,S}$) (S Left Outer θ-Join($D_{S,T}$) T).

Since $t_1, \ldots t_k$ are not all Null, $D_{S,T}$ is TRUE for the values $s_1, \ldots s_n, t_1, \ldots t_k$ and thus these values are a row in S θ-Join($D_{S,T}$) T. Likewise, because $s_1, \ldots s_n$ are not all Null, $C_{R,S}$ is TRUE for the values $r_1, \ldots r_m, s_1, \ldots s_n$. Since the T-values aren't used in $C_{R,S}$, $C_{R,S}$ is also TRUE for the values $\{r_1, \ldots r_m\}$ and $\{s_1, \ldots s_n, t_1, \ldots t_k\}$. Therefore $r_1, \ldots r_m, s_1, \ldots s_n, t_1, \ldots t_k$ is a row in R θ-Join($C_{R,S}$) (S θ-Join($D_{S,T}$) T).

By the associativity of θ-Join, these values also form a row in (R θ-Join($C_{R,S}$) S) θ-Join($D_{S,T}$) T. Since any row in a θ-Join is also a row in the corresponding Left Outer θ-Join, it follows that $r_1, \ldots r_m, s_1, \ldots s_n, t_1, \ldots t_k$ form a row in (R Left Outer θ-Join($C_{R,S}$) S) Left Outer θ-Join($D_{S,T}$) T.

Case 2) $s_1, \ldots s_n$ aren't all Null; $t_1, \ldots t_k$ are all Null.
Let $r_1, \ldots r_m, s_1, \ldots s_n, t_1, \ldots t_k$ be a row in R Left Outer θ-Join($C_{R,S}$) (S Left Outer θ-Join($D_{S,T}$) T).

Because the S-values are not all Null, it follows trivially that $s_1, \ldots s_n, t_1, \ldots t_k$ are also not all Null. Therefore, $C_{R,S}$ is TRUE for $\{r_1, \ldots r_m\}$ and $\{s_1, \ldots s_n, t_1, \ldots t_k\}$. Since the T-values are not used, $C_{R,S}$ is also TRUE for $r_1, \ldots r_m$ and $s_1, \ldots s_n$. So $r_1, \ldots r_m, s_1, \ldots s_n$ is a row in R θ-Join($C_{R,S}$) S and thus in R Left Outer θ-Join($C_{R,S}$).

Because $t_1, \ldots t_k$ are all Null, we know $D_{S,T}$ isn't TRUE for the values $\{s_1, \ldots s_n\}$ and any row in T. Since the R-values aren't used, $D_{S,T}$ also isn't TRUE for the values $r_1, \ldots r_m, s_1, \ldots s_n$ and any row in T. It follows that $r_1, \ldots r_m, s_1, \ldots s_n, t_1, \ldots t_k$ form a row in (R Left Outer θ-Join($C_{R,S}$) S) Left Outer θ-Join($D_{S,T}$).

Case 3) $s_1, \ldots s_n$ are all Null; $t_1, \ldots t_k$ aren't all Null. We'll show that this case couldn't occur.
Let $r_1, \ldots r_m, s_1, \ldots s_n, t_1, \ldots t_k$ be a row in R Left Outer θ-Join($C_{R,S}$) (S Left Outer θ-Join($D_{S,T}$) T).

Since $t_1, \ldots t_k$ aren't all Null, $C_{R,S}$ must be TRUE for $r_1, \ldots r_m$ and some row in S Left Outer θ-Join($D_{S,T}$) T. However, the T-values aren't used so $C_{R,S}$ must be TRUE for $r_1, \ldots r_m$ and some row in S which would mean that $s_1, \ldots s_n$ aren't all Null. Since this contradicts the assumptions, this case couldn't occur.

Case 4) $s_1, \ldots s_n$ are all Null; $t_1, \ldots t_k$ are all Null.
Let $r_1, \ldots r_m, s_1, \ldots s_n, t_1, \ldots t_k$ be a row in R Left Outer θ-Join($C_{R,S}$) (S Left Outer θ-Join($D_{S,T}$) T).

Since $s_1, \ldots s_n, t_1, \ldots t_k$ are all Null, $C_{R,S}$ isn't TRUE for $r_1, \ldots r_m$ and any row in S Left Outer θ-Join($D_{S,T}$) T. Because the T-values aren't used, $C_{R,S}$ also isn't TRUE for $r_1, \ldots r_m$ and any row in S. Thus $r_1, \ldots r_m, s_1, \ldots s_n$ is a row in (R Left Outer θ-Join($C_{R,S}$) S). Since the R-values aren't used in $D_{S,T}$ and $s_1, \ldots s_n$ are all Null, $D_{S,T}$ isn't TRUE for $r_1, \ldots r_m, s_1, \ldots s_n$ and any row in T and therefore $r_1, \ldots r_m, s_1, \ldots s_n, t_1, \ldots t_k$ is a row in (R Left Outer θ-Join($C_{R,S}$) S) Left Outer θ-Join($D_{S,T}$) T.

Hence, any row in R Left Outer θ-Join($C_{R,S}$) (S Left Outer θ-Join($D_{S,T}$) T) is also in (R Left Outer θ-Join($C_{R,S}$) S) θ-Join($D_{S,T}$) T.

In the same way, we'll now show that any row in (R Left Outer θ-Join($C_{R,S}$) S) Left Outer θ-Join($D_{S,T}$) T is also a row in R Left Outer θ-Join($C_{R,S}$) (S Left Outer θ-Join($D_{S,T}$) T). As before, we'll break the proof up into four cases depending upon whether the attribute values $s_1, \ldots s_n$ and $t_1, \ldots t_k$ are all Null or not for the values in the row $r_1, \ldots r_m, s_1, \ldots s_n, t_1, \ldots t_k$.

Case 1) $s_1, \ldots s_n$ aren't all Null; $t_1, \ldots t_k$ aren't all Null.
Let $r_1, \ldots r_m, s_1, \ldots s_n, t_1, \ldots t_k$ be a row in (R Left Outer θ-Join($C_{R,S}$) S) Left Outer θ-Join($D_{S,T}$) T.
Since $s_1, \ldots s_n$ are not all Null, $C_{R,S}$ is TRUE for the values $r_1, \ldots r_m, s_1, \ldots s_n$ and thus these values are a row in R θ-Join($C_{R,S}$) S. Likewise, because $t_1, \ldots t_k$ are not all Null, $D_{S,T}$ is TRUE for the values $\{r_1, \ldots r_m, s_1, \ldots s_n\}$ and $\{t_1, \ldots t_k\}$. Therefore $r_1, \ldots r_m, s_1, \ldots s_n, t_1, \ldots t_k$ is a row in (R θ-Join($C_{R,S}$) S) θ-Join($D_{S,T}$) T.

By the associativity of θ-Join, these values also form a row in R θ-Join($C_{R,S}$) (S θ-Join($D_{S,T}$) T). Since any row in a θ-Join is also a row in the corresponding Left Outer θ-Join it follows that $r_1, \ldots r_m, s_1, \ldots s_n, t_1, \ldots t_k$ form a row in R Left Outer θ-Join($C_{R,S}$) (S Left Outer θ-Join($D_{S,T}$) T).

Case 2) $s_1, \ldots s_n$ aren't all Null; $t_1, \ldots t_k$ are all Null.
Let $r_1, \ldots r_m, s_1, \ldots s_n, t_1, \ldots t_k$ be a row in (R Left Outer θ-Join($C_{R,S}$) S) Left Outer θ-Join($D_{S,T}$) T.

Because $s_1, \ldots s_n$ are not all Null it follows that $s_1, \ldots s_n$ is a row in S and since $t_1, \ldots t_k$ are all Null, we know $D_{S,T}$ isn't TRUE for the values $\{r_1, \ldots r_m, s_1, \ldots s_n\}$ and any row in T. Since the R-values aren't used, $D_{S,T}$ also isn't TRUE for the values $s_1, \ldots s_n$ and any row in T. Thus $s_1, \ldots s_n, t_1, \ldots t_k$ form a row in S Left Outer θ-Join($D_{S,T}$) T.

Also because $s_1, \ldots s_n$ are not all Null, $C_{R,S}$ must be TRUE for $r_1, \ldots r_m$ and $s_1, \ldots s_n$ and since the t-values aren't used, $C_{R,S}$ is also TRUE for $\{r_1, \ldots r_m\}$ and $\{s_1, \ldots s_n, t_1, \ldots t_k\}$. Thus $r_1, \ldots r_m, s_1, \ldots s_n, t_1, \ldots t_k$ form a row in R θ-Join($C_{R,S}$)(S Left Outer θ-Join($D_{S,T}$) T) and therefore also in R Left Outer θ-Join($C_{R,S}$)(S Left Outer θ-Join($D_{S,T}$) T).

Case 3) $s_1, \ldots s_n$ are all Null; $t_1, \ldots t_k$ aren't all Null. We'll show that this case couldn't occur.
Let $r_1, \ldots r_m, s_1, \ldots s_n, t_1, \ldots t_k$ be a row in (R Left Outer θ-Join($C_{R,S}$) S) Left Outer θ-Join($D_{S,T}$) T.

Since $t_1, \ldots t_k$ aren't all Null, $D_{S,T}$ must be TRUE for $r_1, \ldots r_m, s_1, \ldots s_n$ and some row in T. Because the R-values aren't used, $D_{S,T}$ must also be TRUE for $s_1, \ldots s_n$ and some row in T. However, $D_{S,T}$ cannot be TRUE for $s_1, \ldots s_n$ and any row in T because $s_1, \ldots s_n$ are all Null. Thus this case couldn't occur.

Case 4) $s_1, \ldots s_n$ are all Null; $t_1, \ldots t_k$ are all Null.
Let $r_1, \ldots r_m, s_1, \ldots s_n, t_1, \ldots t_k$ be a row in (R Left Outer θ-Join($C_{R,S}$) S) Left Outer θ-Join($D_{S,T}$) T.

Since $s_1, \ldots s_n$ are all Null, $C_{R,S}$ isn't TRUE for $r_1, \ldots r_m$ and any row in S. Because the T-values aren't used, $C_{R,S}$ also isn't TRUE for $r_1, \ldots r_m$ and any row in S Left Outer θ-Join($D_{S,T}$) T and – since $s_1, \ldots s_n, t_1, \ldots t_k$ are all Null – $r_1, \ldots r_m, s_1, \ldots s_n, t_1, \ldots t_k$ is a row in R Left Outer θ-Join($C_{R,S}$) (S Left Outer θ-Join($D_{S,T}$) T).

Hence, any row in (R Left Outer θ-Join($C_{R,S}$) S) Left Outer θ-Join($D_{S,T}$) T is also a row in R Left Outer θ-Join($C_{R,S}$) (S Left Outer θ-Join($D_{S,T}$) T).

We've now shown that R Left Outer θ-Join($C_{R,S}$) (S Left Outer θ-Join($D_{S,T}$) T) = (R Left Outer θ-Join($C_{R,S}$) S) Left Outer θ-Join($D_{S,T}$) T and thereby proved that expressions of these forms are associative.

Proof of non-Distributivity of Left Outer θ-Join over UNION: This will be shown by example. Let Relations R ,S and T each with one attribute – R_1, S_1, and S_1 respectively – have values as below. Further, let $C_{R,S}$ be the comparison expression: $R_1 = S_1$. Note that S and T have the same attribute and are UNION compatible.

For the following we'll use LOθJ to denote Left Outer θ-Join($C_{R,S}$) and U to denote UNION:

R		S		T		R LOθJ (S U T)		(R LOθJ S) U (R LOθJ T)	
R_1		S_1		S_1		R_1	S_1	R_1	S_1
1		1		2		1	1	1	1
								1	Null

Since R Left Outer θ-Join($C_{R,S}$) (S UNION T) $\neq$ (R Left Outer θ-Join($C_{R,S}$) S) UNION (R Left Outer θ-Join($C_{R,S}$) T), Left Outer θ-Join is not distributive over UNION.

Left Outer Equi-Join Properties: Left Outer Equi-Join is not commutative or distributive over UNION. Expressions of the form Left Outer R Equi-Join($C_{R,S}$) (S Left Outer Equi-Join($D_{S,T}$) T) and (R Left Outer Equi-Join($C_{R,S}$) S) Left Outer Equi-Join($D_{S,T}$) T are associative.

Proof of non-Commutivity: This will be shown by example. Let Relations R and S each with one attribute – R_1 and S_1 respectively – have values as below. Further, let $C_{R,S}$ be the comparison expression: $R_1 = S_1$.

R		S		R LEFT OUTER EQUI-JOIN($C_{R,S}$) S		S LEFT OUTER EQUI-JOIN($C_{R,S}$) R	
R_1		S_1		R_1	S_1	S_1	R_1
1		1		1	1	1	1
2		3		2	Null	3	Null

Since R Left Outer Equi($C_{R,S}$) S $\neq$ S Left Outer Equi-Join($C_{R,S}$) R, Left Outer Equi-Join isn't commutative.

Proof of Associativity: This follows because Left Outer Equi-Join is a special case of Left Outer θ-Join. Let R, S, and T be relations where $C_{R,S}$ is a comparison expression between R and S; $D_{S,T}$ is a comparison expression for S and T. Then we have:

R Left Outer Equi-Join($C_{R,S}$) (S Left Outer Equi-Join($D_{S,T}$) T) = (R Left Outer Equi-Join($C_{R,S}$) S) Left Outer Equi-Join($D_{S,T}$) T.

<u>Proof of non-Distributivity of Left Outer Equi-Join over UNION</u>: This will be demonstrated by the same example used for Left Outer θ-Join. Thus let Relations R ,S and T each with one attribute – R_1, S_1, and S_1 respectively – have values as below. Further, let $C_{R,S}$ be the comparison expression: $R_1 = S_1$. Note that S and T have the same attribute and are UNION compatible.

For the following we'll use LOEJ to denote Left Outer Equi-Join($C_{R,S}$) and U to denote UNION:

R
R_1
1

S
S_1
1

T
S_1
2

R LOEJ (S U T)

R_1	S_1
1	1

(R LOEJ S) U (R LOEJ T)

R_1	S_1
1	1
1	Null

Since R Left Outer Equi-Join($C_{R,S}$) (S UNION T) ≠ (R Left Outer Equi-Join($C_{R,S}$) S) UNION (R Left Outer Equi-Join($C_{R,S}$) T), Left Outer Equi-Join is not distributive over UNION.

Left Outer Natural Join (Left Outer Join)

From Chapter 3, we have the following conditions for a row to be in a Left Outer Join.

Let R be a relation with attribute names $R_1, \ldots R_m, C_1, \ldots C_k$ and S a relation with attribute names $S_1, \ldots S_n$, $C_1, \ldots C_k$. The common attributes of R and S are $C_1, \ldots C_k$ and the heading of the result relation of the Left Outer Join of R and S is $R_1, \ldots R_m, S_1, \ldots S_n, C_1, \ldots C_k$. Then, the attribute values $r_1, \ldots r_m, s_1, \ldots s_n, c_1, \ldots c_k$ form a row in the result relation if and only if:

Either 1) $r_1, \ldots r_m, c_1, \ldots c_k, s_1, \ldots s_n$ form a row in (R Join S).
Or 2) The values $r_1, \ldots r_m, c_1, \ldots c_k$ form a row in R but don't appear together in any row of the corresponding Join and $s_1, \ldots s_n$ are all null.

Inference 3.3.3: The Left Outer Join of two relations with no common attributes equals their product.

Proof of Inference 3.3.3: Note that from Inference 3.3.1 that if there are no common attributes in R and S above, then R Join S becomes R TIMES S. Thus the conditions for $r_1, \ldots r_m, s_1, \ldots s_n$ to be a row in the Left Outer Join become:
1) $r_1, \ldots r_m, s_1, \ldots s_n$ form a row in R TIMES S
OR 2) $r_1, \ldots r_m$ form a row in R, but are not in any row of R TIMES S. However, this is not possible.

Hence, the condition for being a row in R Left Outer Join S is precisely the condition for a row being in R TIMES S – thus proving Inference 3.3.3.

This completes the proof of Inference 3.3.3.

Left Outer Join Properties: Left Outer Join is not commutative and not distributive over UNION. It's not generally associative, however the following condition is sufficient to ensure associativity: The adjoining relations have at least one attribute in common, but the relations on the far left and far right of the expression have no attributes in common.

<u>Proof of non-Commutivity of Left Outer Join</u>: This will be demonstrated by example. Let Relations R with attributes A, B and S with attributes A, C have values as below.

Relation R

A	B
1	4
2	5

Relation S

A	C
1	6
3	7

R LEFT OUTER JOIN S

A	B	C
1	4	6
2	5	Null

S LEFT OUTER JOIN R

A	B	C
1	4	6
3	Null	7

Since R Left Outer Join S ≠ S Left Outer Join R, Left Outer Join is not commutative.

Proof of Non Distributivity of Left Outer Join over UNION: This will be demonstrated by example. Let R, S and T be relations with attributes and values as below where T is UNION compatible with S. We'll use LOJ to denote Left Outer Join and U to denote UNION.

R		S			T			R LOJ (S U T)			(R LOJ S) U (R LOJ T)	
B		A	B		A	B		A	B		A	B
1		1	1		1	2		1	1		1	1
											Null	1

Since R LOJ (S U T) ≠ (R LOJ S) U (R LOJ T), Join is not distributive over UNION.

Proof of Associativity of Left Outer Join: We'll prove associativity with the restriction that the adjoining relations have at least one attribute in common, but the relations on the far left and far right have none. Note: See Section 3.3 for examples that don't meet the above restriction and aren't associative.

We'll use the following notation:
r – A set of values for the non-common attributes in R.
C – The set of common attributes for R and S. We assume C has at least one attribute.
c – A set of values for C.
s – A set of values for the non-common attributes in S.
D – The set of common attributes for S and T. We assume D has at least one attribute.
d – A set of values for D.
t – A set of values for the non-common attributes in T.
Combinations such as **csd** denote all the values in c, s and d.
LOJ denotes the Left Outer Join.

We'll say that two rows "**match**" if the common values on a row in relation R equal the common values on a row in relation S. Similarly a row in S may match a row in T. This precludes the common values having any Nulls because Nulls can't equal anything (including another Null).

For a row rcsdt in R LOJ (S LOJ T): If c has a Null it's possible for csd – with sd all Nulls – to be a row in S without being a match for rc. csd is a match for rc if and only if c has no nulls and csd is a row in S. Similarly, dt is a match for csd if and only if d has no nulls and dt is a row in T. Hence, we define our Cases in the proof depending on the values of c, csd, d and dt.

We'll first prove the following Lemma using the preceding notation and, as above, assume that there's at least one attribute in common for R, S and S, T respectively and no attributes in common for R, T.

Lemma 1: If rcsdt is a row in R LOJ (S LOJ T), then rcsd is a row in (R LOJ S).
Proof of Lemma 1: Since rcsdt is a row in R LOJ (S LOJ T), rc is a row in R.
If csd is a row in S and c has no Nulls, then the common values, c, on row csd of S equal the values on row rc of R and thus rcsd is a row in (R Join S) and therefore also in (R LOJ S).
Otherwise, if csd isn't a row in S or c has at least one Null, then there's no row in (S LOJ T) – and thus in S (since R and T have no common attributes) – that matches rc. Hence sdt is set Null in forming R LOJ (S LOJ T). Because no row in S matches rc and sd is all Null, rcsd is a row in R LOJ S thus proving Lemma 1.

To prove associativity, we'll first show that any row in R LOJ (S LOJ T) is also in (R LOJ S) LOJ T:

Case 1) rcsdt is a row in R LOJ (S LOJ T) such that:
csd is a row in S and c has no Nulls; dt is a row in T and d has no Nulls.
By Lemma 1 rcsd is a row in (R LOJ S). Since dt is a row in T and d has no Nulls, the common attributes in S and D – and thus in (R LOJ S) and D – are equal so rcsdt is a row in (R LOJ S) Join T and thus also in (R LOJ S) LOJ T.

Case 2) rcsdt is a row in R LOJ (S LOJ T) such that:
csd is a row in S and c has no Nulls; dt isn't a row in T or d has at least one Null.
Since dt isn't a row in T or d has at least one Null, there's no row in T whose values equal d and thus t is set to Nulls in forming S LOJ T. Hence the row rcsdt has all Nulls for t.
By Lemma 1 rscd is a row in (R LOJ S) that has the attributes D in common with T and thus t is set to Nulls in forming (R LOJ S) LOJ T resulting in rcsd filled out with Nulls for t as above. Hence rcsdt is a row in (R LOJ S) LOJ T.

– Proofs for Section 3.3: Left Outer Natural Join –

Case 3) rcsdt is a row in R LOJ (S LOJ T) such that:
csd isn't a row in S or c has at least one Null.

Since csd isn't a row in S or c has a Null, there's no row in (S LOJ T) where the values of C equal c. Thus sdt are set to all Nulls in forming R LOJ (S LOJ T) and rcsdt consists of rc filled out with Nulls for sdt.

From Lemma 1 rcsd forms a row in (R LOJ S) and since csd isn't a row in S or c has at least one Null, sd is set to all Nulls to form (R LOJ S). Since D has at least one attribute and d is all Nulls there can't be a row in T where the values of D equal d. Thus t is set to all Nulls in forming (R LOJ S) LOJ T that results in the row rc filled out with Nulls for sdt as above so rcsdt is a row in (R LOJ S) LOJ T.

Therefore any row in R LOJ (S LOJ T) is also in (R LOJ S) LOJ T.

In a similar way, we'll now show that any row in (R LOJ S) LOJ T is also in R LOJ (S LOJ T).

We'll first prove the following Lemma that will be used later. We'll use the preceding notation and, as above, assume that there's at least one attribute in common for R, S and S, T respectively and no attributes in common for R, T.

Lemma 2: If rcsdt is a row in (R LOJ S) LOJ T and csd is a row in S, then csdt is a row in (S LOJ T).
Proof of Lemma 2: Since rcsdt is a row in (R LOJ S) LOJ T, rcsd is a row in R LOJ S.
If dt is a row in T and d has no Nulls, then since csd is also a row in S, csdt is a row in S Join T and therefore also in S LOJ T.
Otherwise, if dt isn't a row in T or d has at least one Null, there's no row in T where the D values are equal to their values on row rcsd in R LOJ S and so t are set to all Nulls in forming (R LOJ S) LOJ T. Since the common values for R LOJ S and T are d there's no row in T where the D values are equal to their values on row csd in S. and – since t are all Nulls – csdt is a row in S LOJ T. Thus Lemma 2 is proven.

Case 1) rcsdt is a row in (R LOJ S) LOJ T such that csd is a row in S and c has no Nulls.

By Lemma 2, csdt is a row in (S LOJ T). Because the common attributes for R and (S LOJ T) are in C and since csd is a row in S and c has no Nulls the row rc in R matches row csdt in (S LOJ T) so rcsdt is a row in R Join (S LOJ T) and thus also in R LOJ (S LOJ T).

Case 2) rcsdt is a row in (R LOJ S) LOJ T such that:
csd isn't a row in S or c has at least one Null; dt is a row in T and d has no Nulls. (This case can't occur.)
We'll show this case couldn't occur.

Because csd isn't a row in S or c has at least one Null, there's no row in S with values c to match row rc in R and thus sd are set to Nulls in forming row rcsd from R LOJ S. Since d are all Nulls in R LOJ S, they're also all Nulls in (R LOJ S) LOJ T. This contradicts the assumptions and therefore this case couldn't occur.

Case 3) rcsdt is a row in (R LOJ S) LOJ T such that:
csd isn't a row in S or c has at least one Null; dt isn't a row in T or d has at least one Null.

Because csd isn't a row in S or c has a Null, sd are set to Nulls to form rcsd from (R LOJ S). Since d is all Nulls, t is set to Nulls to form rcsdt from (R LOJ S) LOJ T. Thus rcsdt consists of rc and all Nulls for sdt.

Also, since csd isn't a row in S or c has a Null there's no row in S – and therefore in (S LOJ T) – whose values for C equal the values for C on row rc in R and thus sdt are set to all Nulls to form rcsdt in R LOJ (S LOJ T). Hence rcsdt has rc and all Nulls for sdt as above so rcsdt is a row in R LOJ (S LOJ T).

We've now shown that R LOJ (S LOJ T) = (R LOJ S) LOJ T and thus proved that LOJ is associative. We reiterate that the proof assumes that the adjoining relations R and S as well as S and T have at least one attribute in common but the far left and far right relations, R and T, have no attributes in common.

Inference 3.3.4 for Right Outer Joins:
R Right Outer θ-Join($C_{R,S}$) S = S Left Outer θ-Join($C_{R,S}$) R.
R Right Outer Equi-Join($C_{R,S}$) S = S Left Outer Equi-Join ($C_{R,S}$) R.
R Right Outer Join S (the right outer natural join) = S Left Outer Join R.

Proof of Inference 3.3.4 for Right Outer θ-Join and Right Outer Equi-Join:

Let the attribute names of a relation R be $R_1, \ldots R_m$ and the attribute names of S be $S_1, \ldots S_n$ with no common attributes between R and S. Let $C_{R,S}$ be a comparison expression on some attributes of R and S. Then the attribute values $r_1, \ldots r_m, s_1, \ldots s_n$ form a row in the result relation of R Right Outer θ-Join S with each r_i in the column for R_i and each s_i in the column for S_i if and only if:

Either 1) $r_1, \ldots r_m, s_1, \ldots s_n$ form a row in (R θ-Join($C_{R,S}$) S) with each r_i in the column for R_i and each s_i in the column for S_i.
Or 2) The values $s_1, \ldots s_n$ form a row in S but do not appear together in any row of the corresponding θ-Join and $r_1, \ldots r_m$ are all null.

However, the above are precisely the conditions for a row to be in S Left Outer θ-Join($C_{R,S}$) R. Thus the inference is proved for Right Outer θ-Join and also for Right Outer Equi-Join.

Proof of Inference 3.3.4 for Right Outer Join (the right outer natural join):

Let R be a relation with attribute names $R_1, \ldots R_m, C_1, \ldots C_k$ and S a relation with attribute names $S_1, \ldots S_n$, $C_1, \ldots C_k$. The common attributes of R and S are $C_1, \ldots C_k$ and the heading of the result relation of R Right Outer Natural Join S is $R_1, \ldots R_m, S_1, \ldots S_n, C_1, \ldots C_k$. Then, the attribute values $r_1, \ldots r_m, s_1, \ldots s_n, c_1, \ldots c_k$ form a row in the result relation of R Right Outer Join S with each r_i in the column for R_i, s_i in the column for S_i and c_i in the column for C_i if and only if:
Either 1) $r_1, \ldots r_m, c_1, \ldots c_k, s_1, \ldots s_n$ form a row in (R Join S) with each r_i in the column for R_i, each c_i in the column for C_i and each s_i in the column for S_i.
Or 2) The values $s_1, \ldots s_n, c_1, \ldots c_k$ form a row in S but don't appear together in any row of the corresponding Join and $r_1, \ldots r_m$ are all null.

Since the above are also the conditions for a row to be in S Left Outer Join ($C_{R,S}$) R, the inference is proved for Right Outer Join.

This completes the proof of Inference 3.3.4.

Properties of Right Outer Joins:

The properties of the Right Outer Joins are the same as the Left Outer Joins: They are all non-primitive, non-commutative and not distributive over UNION.

Expressions of the form R Right Outer θ-Join($C_{R,S}$) (S Right Outer θ-Join($D_{S,T}$) T) and (R Right Outer θ-Join($C_{R,S}$) S) Right Outer θ-Join($D_{S,T}$) T and the corresponding expressions for Right Outer Equi-Join are associative.

Right Outer Join (right outer natural join) is not generally associative, however, the following restriction is sufficient to assure associativity for Right Outer Join: The adjoining relations have at least one attribute in common, but the relations on the far left and far right of the expression have no attributes in common.

Proof of Right Outer Join Properties: From Inference 3.3.4 we have the following:
R Right Outer θ-Join($C_{R,S}$) S = S Left Outer θ-Join($C_{R,S}$) R.
R Right Outer Equi-Join($C_{R,S}$) S = S Left Outer Equi-Join($C_{R,S}$) R.
R Right Outer Join S = S Left Outer Join R.

Hence, equivalent Left Outer Joins can replace all three Right Outer Joins and thus the Right Outer Joins have the same properties as the corresponding Left Outer Joins.

Inference 3.3.5: The full outer join of two relations is equal to the UNION of the corresponding left and right outer joins. Thus:

R Full Outer θ-Join($C_{R,S}$) S = (R Left Outer θ-Join($C_{R,S}$) S) UNION (R Right Outer θ-Join($C_{R,S}$) S).
R Full Outer Equi-Join($C_{R,S}$)S=(R Left Outer Equi-Join($C_{R,S}$) S)UNION(R Right Outer Equi-Join($C_{R,S}$) S).
R Full Outer Join S (the full outer natural join) = (R Left Outer Join S) UNION (R Left Outer Join S).

<u>Proof of Inference 3.3.5 For Full Outer θ-Join and Full Outer Equi-Join:</u>

Let the attribute names of a relation R be $R_1, \ldots R_m$ and the attribute names of S be $S_1, \ldots S_n$ with no common attributes between R and S. Let $C_{R,S}$ be a comparison expression on some attributes of R and S. Then the attribute values $r_1, \ldots r_m, s_1, \ldots s_n$ form a row in R Full Outer θ-Join($C_{R,S}$) S if and only if:

Either 1) $r_1, \ldots r_m, s_1, \ldots s_n$ form a row in (R θ-Join($C_{R,S}$) S.
Or 2) The values $r_1, \ldots r_m$ form a row in R, but do not appear together in any row of the corresponding θ-Join and $s_1, \ldots s_n$ are all null.
Or 3) The values $s_1, \ldots s_n$ form a row in S but do not appear together in any row of the corresponding θ-Join and $r_1, \ldots r_m$ are all null.

Conditions 1) OR 2) are necessary and sufficient for the row to be in R Left Outer θ-Join($C_{R,S}$) S; 1) OR 3) for being a row in R Right Outer θ-Join($C_{R,S}$) S. Hence, $r_1, \ldots r_m, s_1, \ldots s_n$ form a row in R Full Outer θ-Join($C_{R,S}$) S if and only if they form a row in R Left Outer θ-Join($C_{R,S}$) S or in R Right Outer θ-Join($C_{R,S}$) S. Thus the Full Outer θ-Join = Left Outer θ-Join UNION Right Outer θ-Join. Also, Full Outer Equi-Join equals Left Outer Equi-Join UNION Right Outer Equi-Join because it's a type of Full Outer θ-Join.

<u>Proof of Inference 3.3.5 for Full Outer Join:</u>

Let R be a relation with attribute names $R_1, \ldots R_m, C_1, \ldots C_k$ and S a relation with attribute names $S_1, \ldots S_n$, $C_1, \ldots C_k$. The common attributes of R and S are $C_1, \ldots C_k$ and the heading of the result relation of the left outer natural join of R and S is $R_1, \ldots R_m, S_1, \ldots S_n, C_1, \ldots C_k$. Then, the attribute values $r_1, \ldots r_m, s_1, \ldots s_n, c_1,$ $\ldots c_k$ form a row in the result relation with each r_i in the column for R_i, s_i in the column for S_i and c_i in the column for C_i if and only if:

Either 1) $r_1, \ldots r_m, c_1, \ldots c_k, s_1, \ldots s_n$ form a row in (R Join S).
Or 2) The values $r_1, \ldots r_m, c_1, \ldots c_k$ form a row in R but don't appear together in any row of the corresponding Join and $s_1, \ldots s_n$ are all null.
Or 3) The values $s_1, \ldots s_n, c_1, \ldots c_k$ form a row in S but don't appear together in any row of the corresponding Join and $r_1, \ldots r_m$ are all null.

Conditions 1) OR 2) are necessary and sufficient for the row to be in R Left Outer Join S; 1) OR 3) for being a row in R Right Outer Join S. Hence $r_1, \ldots r_m, s_1, \ldots s_n, c_1, \ldots c_k$ form a row in R Full Outer Join S if and only if they form a row in R Left Outer Join S or in R Right Outer Join S. Thus the Full Outer Join equals Left Outer Join UNION Right Outer Join.

This completes the proof of Inference 3.3.5.

Properties of the Full Outer Joins: The full outer joins are all non-primitive, commutative, and not distributive over UNION.

Expressions of the form Full Outer θ-Join($C_{R,S}$) (S Full Outer θ-Join($D_{S,T}$) T) and (R Full θ-Join($C_{R,S}$) S) Full θ-Join($D_{S,T}$) T and the corresponding Full Outer Equi-Join expressions are associative.

Full Outer Join is associative with the restriction that the adjoining relations have at least one attribute in common and the relations on the far left and far right of the expression have no attributes in common.

From Inference 3.3.5: The full outer join of two relations is equal to the UNION of the corresponding left and right outer joins. The commutivity of the Full Outer Joins follows from the commutivity of UNION as shown next..

Commutivity of Full Outer θ-Join, Full Outer Equi-Join and Full Outer Join:

R Full Outer θ-Join($C_{R,S}$) S = S Full Outer θ-Join($C_{R,S}$) R.
R Full Outer Equi-Join($C_{R,S}$) S = S Full Outer Equi-Join($C_{R,S}$) R.
R Full Outer Join($C_{R,S}$) S (the full outer natural join) = S Full Outer Join($C_{R,S}$) R.

<u>Proof of Commutivity of the Full Outer θ-Join, Equi-Join and Join</u>: From Inference 3.3.5, we have R Full Outer θ-Join($C_{R,S}$) S = (R Left Outer θ-Join($C_{R,S}$) S) UNION (R Right Outer θ-Join($C_{R,S}$) S). From Inference 3.3.4, this can be written (S Right Outer θ-Join($C_{R,S}$) R) UNION (S Left Outer θ-Join($C_{R,S}$) R) = S Full Outer θ-Join($C_{R,S}$) R.

The commutivity of Full Outer Equi-Join and Full Outer Join is similarly proven.

<u>Proof of non Distributivity of Full Outer θ-Join over UNION</u>: We'll demonstrate this by example. Let relations R, S and T each with one attribute – A, B, and B respectively – have values as below. Let $C_{R,S}$ be the comparison expression A = B. Note that S and T are UNION compatible.

For the following we'll use FOθJ to denote FULL Outer θ-Join($C_{R,S}$) and U to denote UNION.

R		S		T		R FOθJ (S U T)		(R FOθJ S) U (R FOθJ T)	
A		B		B		A	B	A	B
1		1		2		1	1	1	1
						Null	2	1	Null
								Null	2

Since R Full Outer θ-Join($C_{R,S}$) (S UNION T) ≠ (R Full Outer θ-Join($C_{R,S}$) S) UNION (R Full Outer θ-Join($C_{R,S}$) T), Full Outer θ-Join is not distributive over UNION.

<u>Proof of non-Distributivity of Full Outer Equi-Join over UNION</u>: This is demonstrated by the preceding example for Full Outer θ-Join because the example is also a Full Outer Equi-Join.

<u>Proof of non-Distributivity of Full Outer Join over UNION</u>: This will be demonstrated by example. Let R be a relation with one attribute named C; S a relation with attributes A, C. Also, let T have attributes A, C so that T is UNION compatible with S. C is a common attribute of R, S and T. Let these relations have attribute values as in the following table.

For the following we'll use FOJ to denote FULL OUTER JOIN and U to denote UNION.

R		S			T			R FOJ (S U T)		(R FOJ S) U (R FOJ T)	
C		A	C		A	C		A	C	A	C
1		1	1		1	2		1	1	1	1
								1	2	Null	1
										1	2

Since R Full Outer Join(S UNION T) ≠ (R Full Outer Join S) UNION (R Full Outer Join T), Full Outer Join is not distributive over UNION.

<u>Proof that Expressions of the form R Full Outer θ-Join($C_{R,S}$) (S Full Outer θ-Join($D_{S,T}$) T) and (R Full θ-Join($C_{R,S}$) S) Full θ-Join($D_{S,T}$) T are associative.</u>
The proof will use the necessary and sufficient criteria for a row to be in a Full Outer θ-Join.

Let the attribute names of relation R be $R_1, \ldots R_m$ with a row of attribute values denoted by $\{r_1, \ldots r_m\}$; let S be a relation with attribute names $S_1, \ldots S_n$ and attribute values denoted by $\{s_1, \ldots s_n\}$; let $C_{R,S}$ denote a comparison condition on the attributes of R and S. Then the attribute values $r_1, \ldots r_m, s_1, \ldots s_n$ form a row in the result relation if and only if:

Either 1) $r_1, \ldots r_m, s_1, \ldots s_n$ form a row in R θ-Join ($C_{R,S}$) S.
Or 2) $r_1, \ldots r_m$ form a row in R with each r_i in the column for R_i, but do not appear together in any row of the corresponding θ-Join and $s_1, \ldots s_n$ are all null.
Or 3) $s_1, \ldots s_n$ form a row in S with each s_i in the column for S_i, but do not appear together in any row of the corresponding θ-Join and $r_1, \ldots r_m$ are all null.

Let R and S be as above and let T be a relation with attribute names T_1, T_2...T_k with a row of attribute values denoted by $\{t_1, \ldots t_k\}$; let $D_{S,T}$ denote a condition on the attribute values of S and T.

To prove that R Full Outer θ-Join($C_{R,S}$) (S Full Outer θ-Join($D_{S,T}$) T) = (R Full Outer θ-Join($C_{R,S}$) S) Full Outer θ-Join($D_{S,T}$) T, we'll first show that any row in the left expression is also a row in the right one.

We'll break the proof up into eight cases depending upon whether the attribute values $\{r_1, \ldots r_m\}$, $\{s_1, \ldots s_n\}$, and $\{t_1, \ldots t_k\}$ are all Null or not for the values in the row $r_1, \ldots r_m, s_1, \ldots s_n, t_1, \ldots t_k$.

Let $r_1, \ldots r_m, s_1, \ldots s_n, t_1, \ldots t_k$ be a row in R Full Outer θ-Join($C_{R,S}$) (S Full Outer θ-Join($D_{S,T}$) T). We'll show that it's also a row in (R Full Outer θ-Join($C_{R,S}$) S) Full Outer θ-Join($D_{S,T}$) T.

Case 1) $r_1, \ldots r_m$ aren't all Null; $s_1, \ldots s_n$ aren't all Null; $t_1, \ldots t_k$ aren't all Null.

By assumption: $r_1, \ldots r_m, s_1, \ldots s_n, t_1, \ldots t_k$ is a row in R Full Outer θ-Join($C_{R,S}$) (S Full Outer θ-Join($D_{S,T}$) T). To show: $r_1, \ldots r_m, s_1, \ldots s_n, t_1, \ldots t_k$ is a row in (R Full Outer θ-Join($C_{R,S}$) S) Full Outer θ-Join($D_{S,T}$) T.

Since neither $r_1, \ldots r_m$ nor $s_1, \ldots s_n, t_1, \ldots t_k$ are all Null, $C_{R,S}$ is TRUE for $r_1, \ldots r_m$ and $s_1, \ldots s_n, t_1, \ldots t_k$ and thus $r_1, \ldots r_m, s_1, \ldots s_n, t_1, \ldots t_k$ is a row in R θ-Join($C_{R,S}$) (S Full Outer θ-Join($D_{S,T}$) T). Similarly, because neither $s_1, \ldots s_n$ nor $t_1, \ldots t_k$ are all Null, $s_1, \ldots s_n, t_1, \ldots t_k$ is a row in S θ-Join($D_{S,T}$) T. It follows that $r_1, \ldots r_m, s_1, \ldots s_n, t_1, \ldots t_k$ is a row in R θ-Join($C_{R,S}$) (S θ-Join($D_{S,T}$) T) and from the associativity of θ-Join, we know that $r_1, \ldots r_m, s_1, \ldots s_n, t_1, \ldots t_k$ is a row in (R θ-Join($C_{R,S}$) S) θ-Join($D_{S,T}$) T.
Since any row in a θ-Join is also in the corresponding Full Outer θ-Join we have that $r_1, \ldots r_m, s_1, \ldots s_n, t_1, \ldots t_k$ form a row in (R Full Outer θ-Join($C_{R,S}$) S) Full Outer θ-Join($D_{S,T}$) T.

Case 2) $r_1, \ldots r_m$ aren't all Null; $s_1, \ldots s_n$ aren't all Null; $t_1, \ldots t_k$ are all Null.

By assumption: $r_1, \ldots r_m, s_1, \ldots s_n, t_1, \ldots t_k$ is a row in R Full Outer θ-Join($C_{R,S}$) (S Full Outer θ-Join($D_{S,T}$) T). To show: $r_1, \ldots r_m, s_1, \ldots s_n, t_1, \ldots t_k$ is a row in (R Full Outer θ-Join($C_{R,S}$) S) Full Outer θ-Join($D_{S,T}$) T.

Since $r_1, \ldots r_m$ aren't all Null and $s_1, \ldots s_n, t_1, \ldots t_k$ aren't all Null, $C_{R,S}$ is TRUE for $r_1, \ldots r_m$, and $s_1, \ldots s_n, t_1, \ldots t_k$ and, therefore, also TRUE for $r_1, \ldots r_m$, and $s_1, \ldots s_n$. Thus $r_1, \ldots r_m, s_1, \ldots s_n$ is a row in R θ-Join($C_{R,S}$) S and thus also in R Full Outer θ-Join($C_{R,S}$) S. Further, because $t_1, \ldots t_k$ are all Null, $D_{S,T}$ is not TRUE for $s_1, \ldots s_n$ and any row in T and thus not TRUE for $r_1, \ldots r_m, s_1, \ldots s_n$ and any row in T. Hence Thus – since $t_1, \ldots t_k$ are all Null – $r_1, \ldots r_m, s_1, \ldots s_n, t_1, \ldots t_k$ is a row in (R Full Outer θ-Join($C_{R,S}$) S) Left Outer θ-Join($D_{S,T}$) T and therefore in (R Full Outer θ-Join($C_{R,S}$) S) Full Outer θ-Join($D_{S,T}$) T.

Case 3) $r_1, \ldots r_m$ aren't all Null; $s_1, \ldots s_n$ are all Null; $t_1, \ldots t_k$ aren't all Null. (This case can't occur.)

By assumption: $r_1, \ldots r_m, s_1, \ldots s_n, t_1, \ldots t_k$ is a row in R Full Outer θ-Join($C_{R,S}$) (S Full Outer θ-Join($D_{S,T}$) T). To show: This case cannot occur.

Since $r_1, \ldots r_m$ aren't all Null and $s_1, \ldots s_n, t_1, \ldots t_k$ aren't all Null, $C_{R,S}$ must be TRUE for $r_1, \ldots r_m$ and $s_1, \ldots s_n, t_1, \ldots t_k$. However, $C_{R,S}$ can't be TRUE for these values because – by assumption – $s_1, \ldots s_n$ are all Null. Hence, there is a contradiction and this case cannot occur.

Case 4) $r_1, \ldots r_m$ aren't all Null; $s_1, \ldots s_n$ are all Null; $t_1, \ldots t_k$ are all Null.

By assumption: $r_1, \ldots r_m, s_1, \ldots s_n, t_1, \ldots t_k$ is a row in R Full Outer θ-Join($C_{R,S}$) (S Full Outer θ-Join($D_{S,T}$) T). To show: $r_1, \ldots r_m, s_1, \ldots s_n, t_1, \ldots t_k$ is a row in (R Full Outer θ-Join($C_{R,S}$) S) Full Outer θ-Join($D_{S,T}$) T.

Because $r_1, \ldots r_m$ aren't all Null and $s_1, \ldots s_n, t_1, \ldots t_k$ are all Null it follows that $r_1, \ldots r_m, s_1, \ldots s_n, t_1, \ldots t_k$ is a row in R Left Outer θ-Join($C_{R,S}$) (S Full Outer θ-Join($D_{S,T}$) T) and $C_{R,S}$ is not TRUE for $r_1, \ldots r_m$ and any row in S Full Outer θ-Join($D_{S,T}$) T and therefore not TRUE for $r_1, \ldots r_m$ and any row in S. Thus, $r_1, \ldots r_m, s_1, \ldots s_n$ is a row in R Left Outer θ-Join($C_{R,S}$) S and hence also in R Full Outer θ-Join($C_{R,S}$) S.
Since $s_1, \ldots s_n$ are all Null, $D_{S,T}$ can't be TRUE for $s_1, \ldots s_n$ and any row in T. Thus – since $t_1, \ldots t_k$ are all Null – $r_1, \ldots r_m, s_1, \ldots s_n, t_1, \ldots t_k$ is a row in (R Full Outer θ-Join($C_{R,S}$) S) Left Outer θ-Join($D_{S,T}$) T and therefore also in (R Full Outer θ-Join($C_{R,S}$) S) Full Outer θ-Join($D_{S,T}$) T.

Case 5) $r_1, \ldots r_m$ are all Null; $s_1, \ldots s_n$ aren't all Null; $t_1, \ldots t_k$ aren't all Null.

By assumption: $r_1, \ldots r_m, s_1, \ldots s_n, t_1, \ldots t_k$ is a row in R Full Outer θ-Join($C_{R,S}$) (S Full Outer θ-Join($D_{S,T}$) T).
To show: $r_1, \ldots r_m, s_1, \ldots s_n, t_1, \ldots t_k$ is a row in (R Full Outer θ-Join($C_{R,S}$) S) Full Outer θ-Join($D_{S,T}$) T.

Since both the S-values and T-values aren't all Null, $D_{S,T}$ is TRUE for these values and $s_1, \ldots s_n, t_1, \ldots t_k$ form a row in S θ-Join($D_{S,T}$) T and therefore also in S Right Outer θ-Join($D_{S,T}$) T. Because the R-values are all Null, it follows that there is no row in R for which $C_{R,S}$ is TRUE for the R-values in that row and the values $s_1, \ldots s_n, t_1, \ldots t_k$ in S Right Outer θ-Join($D_{S,T}$) T. Thus $r_1, \ldots r_m, s_1, \ldots s_n, t_1, \ldots t_k$ is a row in R Right Outer θ-Join($C_{R,S}$) (S Right Outer θ-Join ($D_{S,T}$) T). However, Right Outer θ-Join is associative, so $r_1, \ldots r_m,$ $s_1, \ldots s_n, t_1, \ldots t_k$ is a row in (R Right Outer θ-Join($C_{R,S}$) S) Right Outer θ-Join($D_{S,T}$) T.
Since any row in a Right Outer θ-Join is also in the corresponding Full Outer Join, we have $r_1, \ldots r_m, s_1,$ $\ldots s_n, t_1, \ldots t_k$ is a row in (R Full Outer θ-Join($C_{R,S}$) S) Full Outer θ-Join($D_{S,T}$) T.

Case 6) $r_1, \ldots r_m$ are all Null; $s_1, \ldots s_n$ aren't all Null; $t_1, \ldots t_k$ are all Null.

By assumption: $r_1, \ldots r_m, s_1, \ldots s_n, t_1, \ldots t_k$ is a row in R Full Outer θ-Join($C_{R,S}$) (S Full Outer θ-Join($D_{S,T}$) T).
To show: $r_1, \ldots r_m, s_1, \ldots s_n, t_1, \ldots t_k$ is a row in (R Full Outer θ-Join($C_{R,S}$) S) Full Outer θ-Join($D_{S,T}$) T.

Since $r_1, \ldots r_m$ are all Null, there is no row in R for which $C_{R,S}$ is TRUE for the values $s_1, \ldots s_n, t_1, \ldots t_k$. and therefore for the values $s_1, \ldots s_n$. Hence $r_1, \ldots r_m, s_1, \ldots s_n$ is a row in R Right Outer θ-Join($C_{R,S}$) S. Because $t_1,$ $\ldots t_k$ are all Null, there's no row in T such that $D_{S,T}$ is TRUE for $s_1, \ldots s_n$ – and thus for R Right Outer θ-Join($C_{R,S}$) S – and the values in that row. So $r_1, \ldots r_m, s_1, \ldots s_n, t_1, \ldots t_k$ is a row in (R Right Outer θ-Join($C_{R,S}$) S) Left Outer θ-Join($D_{S,T}$) T and thus in (R Full Outer θ-Join($C_{R,S}$) S) Full Outer θ-Join($D_{S,T}$) T.

Case 7) $r_1, \ldots r_m$ are all Null; $s_1, \ldots s_n$ are all Null; $t_1, \ldots t_k$ aren't all Null.

By assumption: $r_1, \ldots r_m, s_1, \ldots s_n, t_1, \ldots t_k$ is a row in R Full Outer θ-Join($C_{R,S}$) (S Full Outer θ-Join($D_{S,T}$) T).
To show: $r_1, \ldots r_m, s_1, \ldots s_n, t_1, \ldots t_k$ is a row in (R Full Outer θ-Join($C_{R,S}$) S) Full Outer θ-Join($D_{S,T}$) T.

Since $r_1, \ldots r_m$ are all Null and $s_1, \ldots s_n, t_1, \ldots t_k$ aren't all Null, $r_1, \ldots r_m, s_1, \ldots s_n, t_1, \ldots t_k$ is a row in R Right Outer θ-Join($C_{R,S}$) (S Full Outer θ-Join($D_{S,T}$) T) and $s_1, \ldots s_n, t_1, \ldots t_k$ is a row in (S Full Outer θ-Join($D_{S,T}$) T). Since $s_1, \ldots s_n$ are all Null, $s_1, \ldots s_n, t_1, \ldots t_k$ is a row in (S Right Outer θ-Join($D_{S,T}$) T) and thus $r_1, \ldots r_m, s_1,$ $\ldots s_n, t_1, \ldots t_k$ is a row in R Right Outer θ-Join($C_{R,S}$) (S Right Outer θ-Join($D_{S,T}$) T). By the associativity of Right Outer θ-Join, it's also a row in (R Right Outer θ-Join($C_{R,S}$) S) Right Outer θ-Join($D_{S,T}$) T.
Since any row in a Right Outer θ-Join is a row in the corresponding Full Outer θ-Join $r_1, \ldots r_m, s_1, \ldots s_n, t_1,$ $\ldots t_k$ is a row in (R Full Outer θ-Join($C_{R,S}$) S) Full Outer θ-Join($D_{S,T}$) T.

Case 8) $r_1, \ldots r_m$ are all Null; $s_1, \ldots s_n$ are all Null; $t_1, \ldots t_k$ are all Null. (This case can't occur.)

By assumption: $r_1, \ldots r_m, s_1, \ldots s_n, t_1, \ldots t_k$ is a row in R Full Outer θ-Join($C_{R,S}$) (S Full Outer θ-Join($D_{S,T}$) T).
To show: This case cannot occur.

Since $r_1, \ldots r_m$ are all Null, $r_1, \ldots r_m, s_1, \ldots s_n, t_1, \ldots t_k$ must be a row in R Right Outer θ-Join($C_{R,S}$) (S Full Outer θ-Join($D_{S,T}$) T) where $C_{R,S}$ is not TRUE for any row in R and the row $s_1, \ldots s_n, t_1, \ldots t_k$ in S Full Outer θ-Join($D_{S,T}$) T. This implies that $s_1, \ldots s_n, t_1, \ldots t_k$ must be a row in S Full Outer θ-Join($D_{S,T}$) T that in turn implies that either $s_1, \ldots s_n$ is a row in S or $t_1, \ldots t_k$ is a row in T. However because both $s_1, \ldots s_n$ and $t_1, \ldots t_k$ are all Null neither could be a row in a relation. Thus by contradiction this case cannot occur.

Hence, for all cases 1-8, any row in R Full Outer θ-Join($C_{R,S}$) (S Full Outer θ-Join($D_{S,T}$) T) is also in (R Full Outer θ-Join($C_{R,S}$) S) Full Outer θ-Join($D_{S,T}$) T.

To complete the proof of the associativity of Full Outer θ-Join, we'll show next that any row in (R Full Outer θ-Join($C_{R,S}$)S) Full Outer θ-Join($D_{S,T}$)T is also a row in R Full Outer θ-Join($C_{R,S}$) (S Full Outer θ-Join($D_{S,T}$)T). Let $r_1, \ldots r_m, s_1, \ldots s_n, t_1, \ldots t_k$ be a row in (R Full Outer θ-Join($C_{R,S}$)S) Full Outer θ-Join($D_{S,T}$) T.

Step 1. $r_1, \ldots r_m, s_1, \ldots s_n, t_1, \ldots t_k$ is a row in (R Full Outer θ-Join($C_{R,S}$) S) Full Outer θ-Join($D_{S,T}$) T. This is by assumption.

Step 2. $r_1, \ldots r_m, s_1, \ldots s_n, t_1, \ldots t_k$ is a row in T Full Outer θ-Join($D_{S,T}$) (S Full Outer θ-Join($C_{R,S}$) R).

Proof of Step 2: This follows from Step 1 and the commutivity of Full Outer θ-Join. That is, (R Full Outer θ-Join($C_{R,S}$) S) Full Outer θ-Join($D_{S,T}$) T = T Full Outer θ-Join($D_{S,T}$) (S Full Outer θ-Join($C_{R,S}$) R).

Step 3. $r_1, \ldots r_m, s_1, \ldots s_n, t_1, \ldots t_k$ is a row in (T Full Outer θ-Join($D_{S,T}$) S) Full Outer θ-Join($C_{R,S}$) R.

Proof of Step 3: This follows from Step 2 and the first part of the proof of the associativity of Full Outer θ-Join presented above (Cases 1-8) that a row in T Full Outer θ-Join($D_{S,T}$) (S Full Outer θ-Join($C_{R,S}$) R) is also a row in (T Full Outer θ-Join($D_{S,T}$) S) Full Outer θ-Join($C_{R,S}$) R.

Step 4. $r_1, \ldots r_m, s_1, \ldots s_n, t_1, \ldots t_k$ is a row in R Full Outer θ-Join($C_{R,S}$) (S Full Outer θ-Join($D_{S,T}$) T).

Proof of Step 4: From Step 3 and the commutivity of Full Outer θ-Join, $r_1, \ldots r_m, s_1, \ldots s_n, t_1, \ldots t_k$ is a row in (T Full Outer θ-Join($D_{S,T}$)S) Full Outer θ-Join($C_{R,S}$)R=R Full Outer θ-Join($C_{R,S}$)(S Full Outer θ-Join($D_{S,T}$)T).

Hence, any row in (R Full Outer θ-Join($C_{R,S}$) S) Full Outer θ-Join($D_{S,T}$) T is also a row in R Full Outer θ-Join($C_{R,S}$) (S Full Outer θ-Join($D_{S,T}$) T). This completes the proof that expressions of the form R Full Outer θ-Join($C_{R,S}$) (S Full Outer θ-Join($D_{S,T}$) T) and (R Full Outer θ-Join($C_{R,S}$) S) Full Outer θ-Join($D_{S,T}$) T are associative.

Proof of Associativity of Full Outer Join: We'll prove associativity with the restriction that the adjoining relations have at least one attribute in common, but the relations on the far left and far right have none. Note: See Section 3.3 for examples of Left Outer Joins that don't meet the above restriction and aren't associative. These same relations also serve as examples for Full Outer Join.

Let R, S, and T be relations where: R and S have at least one attribute in common; S and T have at least one attribute in common; R and T have no attributes in common.

We'll use the following notation:
R' – The set of attributes in R.
C – The set of common attributes for R and S. We assume C has at least one attribute.
S' – The set of non common attributes in S.
D – The set of common attributes for S and T. We assume D has at least one attribute.
T' – The set of attributes in T.

Also, let FOJ and FOθJ denote Full Outer Join and Full Outer θ-Join respectively.

We must show that R FOJ (S FOJ T) = (R FOJ S) FOJ T.

First let V be the result relation from RENAME (S, C_1 to $S.C_1, \ldots C_m$ to $S.C_m$, D_1 to $S.D_1, \ldots D_n$ to $S.D_n$). Then define comparison expressions $C_{R,V}$ and $D_{V,T}$ as:
$C_{R,V}$="$C_1=S.C_1, \ldots C_m=S.C_m$" and $D_{V,T}$="$D_1=S.D_1, \ldots D_n=S.D_n$"

Note that R FOJ (S FOJ T) equals R FOθJ($C_{R,V}$) (V FOθJ($C_{V,T}$) T) except that the header has the extra attributes {$S.C_1, \ldots S.C_m$} and {$S.D_1, \ldots S.D_n$}. Hence, performing a Project operation on R'US'UT' to eliminate the extra attributes results in: R FOJ (S FOJ T) = Project[R FOθJ($C_{R,V}$) (V FOθJ($C_{V,T}$) T), R'US'UT'].

Since Full Outer θ-Join is associative, we have R FOJ (S FOJ T)=Project[R FOθJ($C_{R,V}$) (V FOθJ($C_{V,T}$) T), R'US'UT']=Project[(R FOθJ($C_{R,V}$) V) FOθJ($C_{V,T}$) T, R'US'UT']=(R FOJ S) FOJ T.

Hence R FOJ (S FOJ T)=(R FOJ S) FOJ T and Full Outer Join is associative given that the adjacent relations have at least one attribute in common and those on the far left and right have none in common.

Divide

Given a relation R and a relation S – whose attributes are a proper subset of the attributes of R – construct a new relation consisting of rows that form a row in R when concatenated with any row in S. The heading of the new relation will be all the attributes in R that are not in S.

Let R be a relation with attributes $R_1, \ldots R_m, S_1, \ldots S_n$ and let S be a relation with attributes $S_1, \ldots S_n$. Then r_1, $r_2 \ldots r_m$ is a row in R DIVIDEDBY S with each r_i in the column for R_i if and only if:

1) r_1, $r_2 \ldots r_m$ is a row in PROJECT(R, $\{R_1, \ldots R_m\}$) with each r_i in the column for R_i.

AND 2) r_1, $r_2 \ldots r_m$, s_1, $s_2 \ldots s_n$ is a row in R with each r_i in the column for R_i and s_i in the column for S_i for any set of values $s_1, s_2 \ldots s_n$ that is a row in S.

Divide Properties: Divide is not commutative and not associative. It is distributive over UNION.

Proof of non-commutivity of DIVIDEDBY: Let R and S be as above. To evaluate R DIVIDEDBY S, requires that the attributes of S be a proper subset of the attributes of R; that is, there are some attributes in R that are not in S. Similarly, S DIVIDEDBY R, would require that the attributes of R be a proper subset of those of S which isn't possible if S is a proper subset of R. Thus DIVIDEDBY is not commutative.

Proof of non-associativity of DIVIDEDBY: The evaluation of R DIVIDEDBY (S DIVIDEDBY T) requires that T be a subset of S, while the evaluation of (R DIVIDEDBY S) DIVIDEDBY T requires that T be a subset of those attributes in R that are not in S. Since both these requirements cannot be met, DIVIDEDBY is not associative.

Proof of distributivity of DIVIDEDBY over UNION:

Let R be a relation with attributes $R_1, \ldots R_m, S_1, \ldots S_n$ and let S and T each be relations with attributes $S_1, \ldots S_n$ so that S and T are UNION compatible.

Let r_1, $r_2 \ldots r_m$ be a row in R DIVIDEDBY (S UNION T).
Then 1) r_1, $r_2 \ldots r_m$ is a row in PROJECT(R, $\{ R_1, \ldots R_m\}$) and 2) r_1, $r_2 \ldots r_m$, s_1, $s_2 \ldots s_n$ is a row in R for any set of values $s_1, s_2 \ldots s_n$ that is a row in S UNION T. Hence, r_1, $r_2 \ldots r_m$, s_1, $s_2 \ldots s_n$ is a row in R for any set of values $s_1, s_2 \ldots s_n$ that is a row in S or in T. Thus, r_1, $r_2 \ldots r_m$, s_1, $s_2 \ldots s_n$ is a row in R DIVIDEDBY S or in R DIVIDEDBY T and therefore a row in R DIVIDEDBY S UNION R DIVIDEDBY T.

Let r_1, $r_2 \ldots r_m$ be a row in (R DIVIDEDBY S) UNION (R DIVIDEDBY T).
Then 1) r_1, $r_2 \ldots r_m$ is a row in PROJECT(R, $\{ R_1, \ldots R_m\}$) and 2) [r_1, $r_2 \ldots r_m$, s_1, $s_2 \ldots s_n$ is a row in R for any set of values $s_1, s_2 \ldots s_n$ that is a row in S] OR [r_1, $r_2 \ldots r_m$, s_1, $s_2 \ldots s_n$ is a row in R for any set of values $s_1, s_2 \ldots s_n$ that is a row in T.] Thus, r_1, $r_2 \ldots r_m$, s_1, $s_2 \ldots s_n$ is a row in R for any set of values $s_1, s_2 \ldots s_n$ that is a row in S UNION T and, therefore, r_1, $r_2 \ldots r_m$, s_1, $s_2 \ldots s_n$ is a row in R DIVIDEDBY (S UNION T).

Thus, R DIVIDEDBY (S UNION T) = R DIVIDEDBY (S UNION T) and DIVIDEDBY is distributive over UNION.

Proofs for Chapter 4 – Dependence and Decomposition

Functional Dependence (FD): Let X and Y be sets of attributes for some relation, R. Then Y is functionally dependent on X if and only if whenever the X-values in two rows of R are equal, then the Y-values in those two rows are also equal.

Inference 4.1.1: Let X and Y be sets of attributes for some relation, R, such that Y is a subset of X. Then it is always true that X→Y.

Proof of Inference 4.1.1:

We must show that given sets of attributes, X and Y, where Y is a subset of X, then X→Y.

Let the X-values on rows r and s be equal. Then since Y is a subset of X, all the attributes in Y are also attributes in X and have the same values on rows r and s and therefore X→Y.

This completes the proof of Inference 4.1.1.

Inference 4.1.2: Let X, Y and Z be sets of attributes for some relation, R, such that X→Y and Y→Z. Then it is always true that X→Z. This is called a "transitive functional dependency."

Proof of Inference 4.1.2:

We must show that for sets of attributes X, Y and Z: If X→Y and Y→Z, then X→Z. For a set of attributes A and a row r, let A_r denote the values of A on row r.

Assuming X→Y and Y→Z, then for rows r and s: If $X_r = X_s$, then since X→Y we have $Y_r = Y_s$ and because Y→Z, $Z_r = Z_s$. Hence, X→Z.

This completes the proof of Inference 4.1.2.

Inference 4.1.3: Every set of attributes in a relation is functionally dependent on every super key (and thus also on every candidate).

Proof of Inference 4.1.3:

Let X be a super key for some relation, R, and Y be a set of attributes in R. Since X is a super key, it follows that the X-values are different for any two different rows in R. Thus for any two rows, it can never be true that the X-values are the same and the Y-values are different. Thus, Y is functionally dependent on X. The inference is also true for candidate keys because every candidate key is a super key,

This completes the proof of Inference 4.1.3.

Inference 4.1.4: Let X and Y be sets of attributes for some relation. Then there is a non-trivial FD X→Y if and only if there is a non-trivial FD X→Y-X, where Y-X consists of all the attributes in Y but not in X.

Proof of Inference 4.1.4

First, let X→Y and let row_1, row_2 be any two rows for which the X-values are equal.
Since X→Y, the Y-values are equal in these rows and, therefore, so are the values for the attributes in Y-X. Thus, X→Y-X.

Next, let X→Y-X and let row_1, row_2 be any two rows for which the X-values are equal.
Since X→Y-X, the values for the attributes in Y that are not in X are equal in row_1 and row_2 as are the values for Y that are also in X. Hence, X→Y.

This completes the proof of Inference 4.1.4.

Inference 4.1.5: Let X and Y = {Y_1, Y_2, …Y_n} be sets of attributes for some relation, where each Y_i is an attribute. Then X→Y if and only if X→Y_i for each i from 1 to n.

Proof of Inference 4.1.5:

First, assume X→Y. Then let the X-values be the same for any two rows, r and s, in R. Since X→Y, the Y-values on rows r and s are equal and, therefore, the value for Y_i on row r equals the value of Y_i on row s for each i. Hence, X→Y_i for each i from 1 to n.

Next, assume X→Y_i for each i from 1 to n. Since X→Y_i, the values for Y_i on rows r and s are equal and, therefore, the value of Y on row r equals the value of Y on row S. Hence, X →Y.
This completes the proof of Inference 4.1.5.

Inference 4.1.6: Let X and Y = {Y_1, Y_2, …Y_n} be sets of attributes for some relation, where each Y_i is an attribute. If there's a full FD X→Y_i for each i from 1 to n, then there's a full FD X→Y.

Proof of Inference 4.1.6:

Let X→Y_i be full functional dependencies for each i from 1 to n. From Inference 4.1.5, X→{Y_1, Y_2, …Y_n}. We must show that X→{Y_1, Y_2, …Y_n} is full. Let X' be a subset of X such that X'→{Y_1, Y_2, …Y_n}. Then by Inference 4.1.5 X'→Y_i for each i from 1 to n. Since X→Y_i is full, there is no proper subset of X such that X'→Y_i. Therefore X'=X and thus X→{Y_1, Y_2, …Y_n} is a full functional dependency.
This completes the proof of Inference 4.1.6.

We include the following definition of functional dependence for the proof of Armstrong's Axioms.

Functional Dependence (FD): Let X and Y be sets of attributes for some relation, R. Then Y is functionally dependent on X if and only if whenever the X-values in two rows of R are equal, then the Y-values in those two rows are also equal.

Armstrong's Axioms:

Proof: We'll use the definition of FD to prove Axioms 1-3; for 4-7, we'll use Axioms 1-3.

For a set of attributes A and a row r, let A_r denote the values of A on row r.

1. Reflexivity: If Y is a subset of X, then X→Y.
This was shown in Inference 4.1.1.

2. Augmentation: If X→Y, then XUZ→YUZ.

Assuming X→Y we'll show that for rows r and s, if (XUZ)$_r$ = (XUZ)$_s$, then (YUZ)$_r$ = (YUZ)$_s$.
If (XUZ)$_r$ = (XUZ)$_s$, then each attribute value in (XUZ)$_r$ equals the value of the same attribute in (XUZ)$_s$ and thus X_r = X_s and Z_r = Z_s. By the assumption that X→Y, it follows that Y_r = Y_s. Since Y_r = Y_s and Z_r = Z_s. we have (YUZ)$_r$ = (YUZ)$_s$. Therefore XUZ→YUZ.

3. Transitivity: If X→Y and Y→Z, then X→Z.
This was shown in Inference 4.1.2.

4. Self Determination: X→X.
This is a special case of 1.

5. Decomposition: If X→YUZ, then X→Y and X→Z.
Assume X→YUZ. By 1, YUZ→Y and YUZ→Z. By 3, X→Y and X→Z.

6. Union: If X→Y and X→Z, then X→ YUZ.
Assume X→Y and X→Z. Using X→Z and 2, X→ XUZ. Using X→Y and 2, XUZ→YUZ. By 3, X→ XUZ and XUZ→YUZ imply X→ YUZ.

7. Composition: If X→Y and Z→W, then XUZ→YUW.
Assume X→Y and Z→W. By 2, XUZ→YUZ and YUZ→ YUW. By 3, XUZ→YUW.

This completes the proof of Armstrong's Axioms.

Multivalued Dependency (MVD): Let R be a Relation whose attributes are partitioned into sets X, Y and Z such that each attribute of R is in exactly one of these sets. Then Y is multidependent on X if and only if for any two rows, r and s, with the same X-value, the group of Y-values from all rows with the same X and Z values as r is identical to the group of Y-values from all rows with the same X and Z values as s.

Inference 4.2.1 Let the attributes of a relation R be partitioned into X, Y and Z such that each attribute of R is in exactly one of these attribute sets. Then $\mathbf{X \twoheadrightarrow Y}$ if and only if: Any Y-value and Z- value that appear on rows with the same X-value also appear together on a row with that X-value. That is, if Y_1 appears on a row with X_1, and Z_1 appears on a row with X_1, then X_1, Y_1, and Z_1 appear on a row together.

Proof of Inference 4.2.1:

To prove the "only if" part of the inference, assume $\mathbf{X \twoheadrightarrow Y}$:
Let X_1, Y_1, Z_r appear on a row r and X_1, Y_s, Z_1 appear on row s.

By assumption, $X \twoheadrightarrow Y$, so the group of Y-values from all rows with X-value X_1 and Z-value Z_r is identical to the group of Y-values from all rows with X-value X_1 and Z-value Z_1. Since Y_1 is in the group of Y-values from all rows with values X_1 and Z_r it must also be in the group of all Y-values from all rows with values X_1 and Z_1. Thus X_1, Y_1, and Z_1 appear on a row together.

To prove the "if" part of the inference, assume that if Y_1 appears on a row with X_1, and Z_1 appears on a row with X_1, then X_1, Y_1, and Z_1 appear on a row together:
Let r be a row with X-value X_1 and Z-value Z_r. Let s be a row with values X_1 and Z_s.

1) Let Y_1 be in the group of Y-values for all the rows with values X_1 and Z_r. Then Y_1 appears on a row with X_1, and Z_s appears on a row with X_1. Thus, by assumption, X_1, Y_1, and Z_s appear on a row together. Hence Y_1 is in the group of Y-values for all the rows with values X_1 and Z_s.

2) Let Y_1 be in the group of Y-values for all the rows with values X_1 and Z_s. Then Y_1 appears on a row with X_1, and Z_r appears on a row with X_1. Thus, by assumption, X_1, Y_1, and Z_r appear on a row together. Hence Y_1 is in the group of Y-values for all the rows with values X_1 and Z_r.

1) and 2) above show that for any two rows, r and s, with the same X-value, the group of Y-values from all rows with the same X and Z values as r is identical to the group of Y-values from all rows with the same X and Z values as s and thus by definition $X \twoheadrightarrow Y$.

This completes the proof of Inference 4.2.1.

Inference 4.2.2: Let R be a Relation and let the attributes of R be partitioned into subsets X and Y such that each attribute of R is in exactly one of these attribute sets. Then it is always true that $X \twoheadrightarrow Y$. This MVD is said to be a trivial multivalued dependency.

Proof of Inference 4.2.2:

Let r and s be any two rows with the same X-value. Then – because there aren't any Z-values – the group of Y-values from all rows with the same X -values as r is the group of all Y-values with the same X-value as s and thus $X \twoheadrightarrow Y$.

This completes the proof of Inference 4.2.2.

Inference 4.2.3: FDs whose determinant and dependent have no attributes in common are also MVDs.

Proof: Assume X and Y are sets of attributes for some relation, R, where X and Y have no attributes in common and $X \to Y$; let Z be all the attributes of R that are not in X or Y.

R is a Relation whose attributes are partitioned into sets X, Y and Z such that each attribute of R is in exactly one of these sets. Since $X \to Y$, the group of Y-values from all rows with the same X-value is a single value. Thus – though the Z-values are irrelevant – we can state: for any two rows, r and s, with the same X-value, the group of Y-values from all rows with the same X and Z values as r is identical to the group of Y-values from all rows with the same X and Z values as s. Thus, the FD $X \to Y$ is an MVD.

This completes the proof of Inference 4.2.3.

Inference 4.2.4: For any non-trivial FD X→Y, the modified FD X→Y-X is an MVD. Note that if X and Y have no attributes in common, Y = Y-X.

Proof of Inference 4.2.4:
From Inference 4.1.4, for any non trivial FD X→Y it is also true that there's a non trivial FD X→Y-X. For this modified FD, the determinant and dependent have no attributes in common. Hence, from Inference 4.2.3, the modified FD X→Y-X is an MVD.
This completes the proof of Inference 4.2.4.

Inference 4.3.1: Let X, Y, Z be subsets of the attributes of a relation R, where each attribute is in at least one of these subsets. Then any row in R is also a row in PROJECT(R, XUY) JOIN PROJECT(R, XUZ).

Proof of Inference 4.3.1:
Let X, Y and Z be subsets of the attributes of a relation R such that each attribute is in at least one of these subsets. Let X_1, Y_1, Z_1 be sets of values for X, Y, Z such that $X_1UY_1UZ_1$ form a row in R. Then X_1UY_1 and X_1UZ_1 form rows in PROJECT(R, XUY) and PROJECT(R, XUZ) respectively. The values of any common attributes for the rows X_1UY_1 and X_1UZ_1 must be equal because the values are on the same row in R. Hence $X_1UY_1UZ_1$ form a row in PROJECT(R, XUY) JOIN PROJECT(R, XUZ).
This completes the proof of Inference 4.3.1.

Heath's Theorem (form 1): Let X, Y, and Z be subsets of the attributes of a relation, R, such that each attribute is in at least one of these subsets. If R satisfies the FD X→Y, then R = PROJECT(R, XUY) JOIN PROJECT(R, XUZ). That is, R is non-loss decomposable into its projections on XUY and XUZ.

Proof of Heath's Theorem (form 1):
Let X, Y, and Z be subsets of the attributes of a relation, R, such that each attribute is in at least one of these subsets and let R satisfy the FD X→Y. From Inference 4.3.1, we know that any row in R is a row in PROJECT(R, XUY) JOIN PROJECT(R, XUZ).
Next, let X_1, Y_1, Z_1 be sets of values for X, Y, Z such that $X_1UY_1UZ_1$ forms a row in PROJECT(R, XUY) JOIN PROJECT(R, XUZ). It follows that X_1UY_1 forms a row in PROJECT(R, XUY) and X_1UZ_1 forms a row in PROJECT(R, XUZ). Hence, X_1UY_1 appears on some row of R as does X_1UZ_1. Since X→Y, the only Y-value that can appear on a row with X_1 is Y_1. Thus, the only Y-value that can appear on a row with X_1UZ_1 is Y_1 and therefore $X_1UY_1UZ_1$ forms a row in R.
This completes the proof of Heath's Theorem.

Inference 4.3.2: Let R be a relation with attribute sets X and Y' such that FD X→Y'. If we let Y=Y' - X and let Z consist of the attributes of R that aren't in X or Y, then each attribute in R appears in exactly one of the sets X, Y, Z and – from Inference 4.1.4 – R satisfies the FD X→Y.

Proof of Inference 4.3.2: The proof is in the statement of the inference.

We repeat Heath's Theorem below for use in the proof of Inference 4.3.3.

Heath's Theorem: Let X, Y, and Z be subsets of the attributes of a relation, R, such that each attribute is in exactly one of these sets. If R satisfies the FD X→Y, then R = PROJECT(R, XUY) JOIN PROJECT(R, XUZ). That is, R is non-loss decomposable into its projections on X, Y and X, Z.

Inference 4.3.3: The converse of Heath's theorem is not true. That is, if R = PROJECT(R, XUY) JOIN PROJECT(R, XUZ) it doesn't necessarily follow that X→Y.

Proof of Inference 4.3.3: The proof consists of an example as follows.

Let R be a relation that lists the refrigerator options for a manufacturer. That is, each row in R represents a combination of options that may be ordered for a refrigerator. Let R have attributes X = Freezer location, Y = Size, Z = Color. It's the company's policy that a refrigerator may be ordered with any combination of options. That is, we have the constraint that if the sets of values X_1, Y_1, Z_1 for X, Y, Z each appear on some row they must appear on a row together. (continued on next page)

First we'll prove that R = PROJECT(R, XUY) JOIN PROJECT(R, XUZ).

From Inference 4.3.1, we know that any row in R is also a row in PROJECT(R, XUY) JOIN PROJECT(R, XUZ). We must show that any row in PROJECT(R, XUY) JOIN PROJECT(R, XUZ) is also a row in R.

Let X_1, Y_1, Z_1 be sets of values for X, Y, Z such that $X_1UY_1UZ_1$ form a row in PROJECT(R, XUY) JOIN PROJECT(R, XUZ). It follows that X_1UY_1 is a row in PROJECT(R, XUY) and X_1UZ_1 is a row in PROJECT(R, XUZ) and thus X_1, Y_1, Z_1 each appear on some row in R. By the aforementioned constraint, X_1, Y_1, Z_1 must form a row in R.

Hence we've proven that R = PROJECT(R, XUY) JOIN PROJECT(R, XUZ).

Next, we'll demonstrate that there's no FD X→Y.

Assume: Top, Bot are values for X; 18, 21 are values for Y; White, Black are values for Z. Then the constraint is satisfied in the table to the right because the rows represent every possible combination of options. Further, we note that Top appears on a row with 18 and also with 21. Hence there are two rows in R having the same X-value but two different Y-values and, therefore, it's not true that FD X→Y.

X	Y	Z
Top	18	White
Top	18	Black
Top	21	White
Top	21	Black
Bot	18	White
Bot	18	Black
Bot	21	White
Bot	21	Black

This completes the proof of Inference 4.3.3.

Fagin's Theorem: Let X, Y, and Z be subsets of the attributes of a relation, R, such that each attribute is in exactly one of these subsets. Then R satisfies the MVD X→→Y|Z if and only if R = PROJECT(R, XUY) JOIN PROJECT(R, XUZ).

Proof of Fagin's Theorem:

Let X, Y, and Z be subsets of the attributes of a relation, R, such that each attribute is in exactly one of these subsets.

First we'll prove the "only if" part of the theorem; that is, we'll assume that MVD X→→Y | Z and show that R = PROJECT(R, XUY) JOIN PROJECT(R, XUZ).

From Inference 4.3.1, we know that any row in R is a row in PROJECT(R, XUY) JOIN PROJECT(R, XUZ). Next, let X_1, Y_1, Z_1 be values for X, Y, Z such that $X_1UY_1UZ_1$ forms a row in PROJECT(R, XUY) JOIN PROJECT(R, XUZ). It follows that X_1UY_1 forms a row in PROJECT(R, XUY) and X_1UZ_1 forms a row in PROJECT(R, XUZ). Hence, X_1UY_1 and X_1UZ_1 each appear on some row of R. Since X→→Y | Z, we know from Inference 4.2.1 that "if Y_1 appears on a row with X_1, and Z_1 appears on a row with X_1, then X_1, Y_1, and Z_1 appear on a row together." Therefore, $X_1UY_1UZ_1$ forms a row in R.

Next we'll prove the "if" part of the theorem; that is, we'll assume that R = PROJECT(R, XUY) JOIN PROJECT(R, XUZ) and show that MVD X→→Y|Z. We'll use Inference 4.2.1 and show that if Y_1 appears on a row with X_1, and Z_1 appears on a row with X_1, then X_1, Y_1, and Z_1 appear on a row together.

Let Y_1 appear on some row with X_1 and Z_1 also appear on some (possibly different) row with X_1 in R. Then X_1UY_1 and X_1UZ_1 form rows in PROJECT(R, XUY) and PROJECT(R, XUZ) respectively and $X_1UY_1UZ_1$ forms a row in PROJECT(R, XUY) JOIN PROJECT(R, XUZ). However, by assumption every row in PROJECT(R, XUY) JOIN PROJECT(R, XUZ) is a row in R and thus $X_1UY_1UZ_1$ forms a row in R. Hence, X_1, Y_1, and Z_1 appear on a row together and, by Inference 4.2.1, MVD X→→Y|Z.

This completes the proof of Fagin's Theorem.

For convenience we repeat the following definitions to be used in the proof of Inference 4.3.4:

Independently Updateable: The set of projections in a non-loss decomposition is said to be "independently updateable" if the join of the projections never contains a violation of a functional dependency in the original relation. That is, there isn't any possibility that there could be values in a projection that – when joined with the other projections – could result in a violation of an FD in the resulting join.

Dependency Preservation: The projections of a relation are said to be "dependency preserving" if all the functional dependencies in the original relation can be constructed from the FDs in the projections by using Armstrong's Axioms (see Section 4.1).

Next, we'll state and prove a Lemma that will be used in the proof of Inference 4.3.4.

Lemma 4: Let $R_1, \ldots R_n$ be relations and let $X \rightarrow Y$ be a functional dependency in R_i for some i from 1 to n. Then $X \rightarrow Y$ is an FD in R_1 Join $R_2 \ldots$ Join R_n.

Proof of Lemma 4: Since Join is commutative and associative, we can assume without loss of generality that i=1. Let $\{R'_1, \ldots R'_n\}$ be an occurrence of $\{R_1, \ldots R_n\}$ and let R'_1 Join $R'_2 \ldots$ Join R'_n contain rows with values X_1, Y_1 and X_1, Y_2. By the General Definition of Join (Section 3.3), the values on a row in R'_1 Join R'_2 $\ldots$ Join R'_n that correspond to the attributes in R_1 must form a row in R_1. Thus values X_1, Y_1 and X_1, Y_2 are each on a row in R'_1 and since $X \rightarrow Y$ for R_1 it follows that $Y_1 = Y_2$ and therefore $X \rightarrow Y$ for R_1 Join R_2 $\ldots$ Join R_n. This completes the proof of Lemma 4.

Inference 4.3.4: The projections that form a non-loss, dependency preserving decomposition are independently updateable.

Proof of Inference 4.3.4:

Let R be a relation with a non-loss, dependency preserving decomposition $\{R_1, \ldots R_n\}$. We must show that the join of these projections never contains a violation of a functional dependency in R.

By Lemma 4 above, every FD that's in any of the relations $R_1, \ldots R_n$ is also in R_1 Join $R_2 \ldots$ Join R_n. Thus all the FDs in $R_1, \ldots R_n$ are also in $R = R_1$ Join $R_2 \ldots$ Join R_n and since the decomposition is dependency preserving, it follows that all the FDs in R can be constructed from the FDs in the projections by using Armstrong's Axioms. Hence, the join of the relations can have no violation of the FDs and – by definition – the projections $R_1, \ldots R_n$ are Independently Updateable.

This completes the proof of Inference 4.3.4.

Theorem 4.4.2: Algorithm 4.4.1 correctly determines if a decomposition is non-loss.

Proof of Theorem 4.4.2: We omit this proof and refer the reader to reference [Ul].

Inference 4.4.3: Let R be a relation and let X_1, X_2 ...X_n be subsets of its attributes. Then any row in the projection of R on the union of these subsets is also a row in the joins of the individual projections. That is, any row in Project (R, $X_1 \cup$ ...X_n) is also a row in the Project(R, X_1) ... JOIN Project(R, X_n).

Proof of Inference 4.4.3:

By the "General Definition of Join" in Chapter 3, we know that Project(R, X_1) ...Join Project(R, X_n):
1) Has all the attributes A_1, ...A_m where each A_i appears in at least one of Project(R, X_1), ...Project(R, X_n)
AND
2) Consists of all the rows (a_1, ...a_m) where the values in {a_1, ...a_m} corresponding to the attributes of Project(R, X_i) form a row in Project(R, X_i) for any i.

Project(R, $X_1 \cup$ ...X_n) has all the attributes that appear in at least one of Project(R, X_1) ... JOIN Project(R, X_n) and thus satisfies 1) above.

Let (a_1, ...a_m) be a row in Project (R, $X_1 \cup$ ...X_n). Then, by the definition of projection, a_1, ...a_m appear together on a row in R. Thus all the values in {a_1, ...a_m} corresponding to the attributes in X_i appear on a row together in R and thus form a row in Project(R, X_i) and therefore (a_1, ...a_m) satisfies 2) above.

Hence, by the General Definition of Join, (a_1, ...a_m) is a row in Project(R, X_1) ...Join Project(R, X_n).

This completes the proof of Inference 4.4.3.

Inference 4.4.4: Let R be a relation and let X_1, X_2 ...X_n be subsets of its attributes such that every attribute in R appears in at least one of these subsets. Then any row in R is also a row in the joins of the individual projections. Proof: This is a special case of Inference 4.4.3 where Project(R, $X_1 \cup$ ...X_n) = R.

Inference 4.4.5: Let R be a relation and let X_1, X_2 ...X_n be subsets of its attributes where one of the subsets, X_i, is the set of all the attributes in R. Then R satisfies JD *(X_1, X_2... X_n).

Proof of Inference 4.4.5:

We must show that R is equal to the join of its projections on X_1, X_2 ...X_n. By Inference 4.4.4, any row in R is also a row in Project(R, X_1) Join Project(R, X_2) ...Join Project(R, X_n). We must show that any row in Project(R, X_1) Join Project(R, X_2) ...Join Project(R, X_n) is also a row in R.

Since Join is commutative and associative, we can assume that X_1 is the set of all attributes in R and we can express the join of all the projections as Project(R, X_1) Join (Project(R, X_2) ...Join Project(R, X_n)). Because X_1 contains all the attributes of R, this equals R Join (Project(R, X_2) ...Join Project(R, X_n)).

By the General Definition of Join in Chapter 3, we know that R Join (Project(R, X_2) ...Join Project(R, X_n)):
1) Has attributes A_1, ...A_m where each A_i appears in at least one of R and (Project(R, X_2) ...Join Project(R, X_n)). Since R has all the attributes, {A_1, ...A_m} must contain all the attributes in R.
AND
2) Consists of all the rows (a_1, ...a_m) where the values in {a_1, ...a_m} corresponding to the attributes of R and (Project(R, X_2) ...Join Project(R, X_n)) are rows in R and (Project(R, X_2) ...Join Project(R, X_n)) respectively.

Since the values in {a_1 ...a_m} correspond to the attributes in R, (a_1 ...a_m) is a row in R

This completes the proof of Inference 4.4.5.

Inference 4.4.6: Let the attributes of a relation R be partitioned into subsets X, Y, Z such that each attribute is in exactly one of these subsets. Then R satisfies JD*(XUY, XUZ) if and only if X→→Y| Z.

Proof of Inference 4.4.6:

By the definition of JD, R satisfies JD*(XUY, XUZ) if and only if R = Project(R, XUY) Join Project(R, XUZ). Inference 4.4.6 then follows from Fagin's Theorem.

This completes the proof of Inference 4.4.6.

Proofs for Chapter 5 – Normalization

We repeat the following definition for use in the proof of Inference 5.2.1:

Second Normal Form (2NF): A relation is in Second Normal Form if and only if every informational attribute is fully functionally dependent on all candidate keys.

Inference 5.2.1: A relation is in 2NF if and only if there is no informational attribute that is functionally dependent on just part of a candidate key.

Proof of Inference 5.2.1 Let X be a candidate key and Y be an informational attribute.

First, assume that every informational attribute is fully functionally dependent on all candidate keys. Then, by assumption, Y is fully functionally dependent on X. Since X and Y are arbitrary, it follows that there is no informational attribute that is functionally dependent on just part of a candidate key.

Next, assume that there is no informational attribute that is functionally dependent on just part of a candidate key. From Inference 4.1.3, every set of attributes in a relation is functionally dependent on every super key. Thus Y is functionally dependent on the candidate key X. Since, by assumption, Y cannot be functionally dependent on just part of a candidate key, it must be fully functionally dependent on X. Since X and Y are arbitrary, it follows that every informational attribute is fully functionally dependent on all candidate keys.

This completes the proof of Inference 5.2.1.

We repeat the following definition for use in the inferences that follow.

Third Normal Form (3NF): A relation is in Third Normal Form if and only if every determinant of an informational attribute in a non-trivial full functional dependency is a candidate key.

Inference 5.3.1: A relation that's in 3NF is also in 2NF.

Proof of Inference 5.3.1

Let R be a relation in 3NF with an informational attribute A and a candidate key X. We must show that A is fully functionally dependent on X. By Inference 4.1.3, there's an FD $X \to A$ and since A is informational it's not an attribute in X so $X \to A$ is non trivial. Let X' be a subset of X such that $X' \to A$ is a full functional dependency. Then X' is a determinant of an informational attribute in a non-trivial full functional dependency and – since R is in 3NF – X' must be a candidate key. Thus X=X' and A is fully functionally dependent on X.

This completes the proof of Inference 5.3.1

Inference 5.3.2: A relation is in Third Normal Form if and only if every determinant of an informational attribute in a non-trivial functional dependency is a super key.

Proof of Inference 5.3.2

First, we'll assume that for a relation R, every determinant of an informational attribute in a non-trivial functional dependency is a super key and show that R is in 3NF. We must show that every determinant of an informational attribute in a non-trivial full functional dependency is a candidate key.

Let R be a relation with a set of attributes X and an informational attribute Y such that there is a non-trivial full functional dependency $X \to Y$. Then, by assumption, X is a super key. Let X' be any candidate key that is a subset of X. Since X' is a candidate key, we know from Inference 4.1.3 that $X' \to Y$. Since $X \to Y$ is a full functional dependency, there is no proper subset of X on which Y is functionally dependent. Hence X = X' and X is a candidate key.

Next, we'll assume R is in 3NF; that is, every determinant of an informational attribute in a non-trivial full functional dependency is a candidate key. We must show that every determinant of an informational attribute in a non-trivial functional dependency is a super key.

Let R be a relation with a set of attributes X and an informational attribute Y such that there is a non-trivial functional dependency X→Y. Let X' be a subset of X such that X'→Y is a non-trivial full functional dependency. Then, by assumption, X' is a candidate key. Since X' is a subset of X, X is a super key.

This completes the proof of Inference 5.3.2

Inference 5.3.3: A relation is in Third Normal Form if and only if every determinant of a set of informational attributes in a non-trivial functional dependency is a super key.

Proof of Inference 5.3.3:

First, we'll assume that for a relation R, every determinant of a set of informational attributes in a non-trivial functional dependency is a super key and show that R is in 3NF. We must show that every determinant of an informational attribute in a non-trivial full functional dependency is a candidate key.

Let a relation R have set a of attributes X and an informational attribute Y where X→Y is a non trivial full functional dependency. Then X→{Y} is a non-trivial functional dependency and by assumption X is a super key. Let X' be a subset of X that's a candidate key. Then by inference 4.1.3 X'→Y. Since the dependency X→Y is full, there's no proper subset of X such that X'→Y. Thus X'=X and X is a candidate key.

Next, we'll assume that R is in 3NF; that is, every determinant of an informational attribute in a non trivial full functional dependency is a candidate key. We must show that every determinant of a set of informational attributes in a non-trivial functional dependency is a super key.

Let R be a relation with a set of attributes X and a set of informational attributes $Y = \{Y_1, Y_2, \ldots Y_n\}$ such that there is a non-trivial functional dependency X→Y. From Inference 4.1.5 we know that $X→Y_i$ for each i from 1 to n. Since X→Y is non-trivial, there is at least one attribute in Y, say Y_k, that isn't an attribute in X so $X→Y_k$ is non-trivial. Let X' be a subset of X such that $X'→Y_k$ is a full dependency. Then, by assumption X' is a candidate key and therefore X is a super key.

This completes the proof of Inference 5.3.3.

Inference 5.3.4: A relation is not in 3NF if there is an informational attribute, A, that's fully functionally dependent on a set of attributes, X, that isn't a candidate key and A isn't an attribute in X.

Proof of Inference 5.3.4

Let X be a set of attributes that isn't a candidate key and A be an informational that isn't an attribute in X such that X→Y is a full functional dependency.

Since A isn't an attribute in X, X→Y is a non-trivial full functional dependency that violates the definition of 3NF because, by assumption, X isn't a candidate key.

This completes the proof of Inference 5.3.4

For convenience, we repeat the following algorithm that is used in Theorem 5.3.6:

Algorithm 5.3.5: The Dependency Preserving Decomposition Algorithm: Let F be a set of functional dependencies that is a minimal cover (see Section 4.1) for a relation R. Then let the decomposition consist of all the projections Project(R, X $\cup$ Y) where X$\rightarrow$Y is in F.

We'll use the following Lemma in the two proofs that follow it.

Lemma 5: Let X and A be subsets of attributes in a relation R. If X$\rightarrow$A is a full FD, then X is a candidate key in Project(R, X $\cup$ A).

Proof of Lemma 5: X must have a different value on every row of Project(R, X $\cup$ A) for if it had the same value on two rows, then the value of A would also be the same and the rows would be identical. Hence X is a super key. Since X$\rightarrow$A is a full functional dependency, there is no proper subset of X that is also a super key. Thus X must be a candidate key. This completes the proof of Lemma 5.

Theorem 5.3.6: The Dependency Preserving Decomposition Algorithm yields a dependency preserving decomposition into 3NF.

Proof of Theorem 5.3.6:

Let $\{R_1, \quad R_n\}$ be a set of projections of a relation R formed by applying the dependency preserving algorithm.

First, since the functional dependencies in the decomposition contain a minimal cover, all the FDs in the original relation can be constructed from the FDs in the decomposition. Thus, by definition, the decomposition is dependency preserving.

Next we'll show that each projection in the decomposition is in 3NF:

Let R_k = Project(R, X $\cup$ A) be a projection in the decomposition. By the definition of minimal cover, X$\rightarrow$A is a full functional dependency and A contains just one attribute. Let Y$\rightarrow$B be a non-trivial full functional dependency in R_k where B consists of just one informational attribute. We must show that Y is a candidate key.

By Lemma 5, X is a candidate key for R_k. Since B is an informational attribute, it can't be part of the candidate key X and therefore must be a part of A. However, A and B both contain just one attribute so A=B. Because Y$\rightarrow$B, it follows from the fact that A=B that Y$\rightarrow$A is a non-trivial full functional dependency. Also, Y is a set of attributes from X $\cup$ A that doesn't contain A and, thus, Y is a subset of X. However, since X$\rightarrow$A is a full functional dependency, Y cannot be a proper subset of X and therefore Y = X. Since X is a candidate key, Y must also be a candidate key for R_k. Thus R_k is in 3NF.

This completes the proof of Theorem 5.3.6.

Inference 5.3.7: Let X$\rightarrow$A$_1$, ...X$\rightarrow$A$_n$ be some of the FDs in a minimal cover, F, for a relation R. Then modifying the Dependency Preserving Algorithm for F by replacing Project(R, X $\cup$ A$_1$), ...Project(R, X $\cup$ A$_n$) with Project(R, X $\cup$ {A$_1$, ...A$_n$}) still yields a dependency preserving decomposition into 3NF.

Proof of Inference 5.3.7

The functional dependencies are preserved in the modified algorithm because Project(R, X $\cup$ {A$_1$, ...A$_n$}) contains all the attributes involved in the functional dependencies X$\rightarrow$A$_1$, ...X$\rightarrow$A$_n$. All that remains to be shown is that Project(R, X $\cup$ {A$_1$, ...A$_n$}) is in 3NF.

First we note that by definition X$\rightarrow$A$_1$, ...X$\rightarrow$A$_n$ are full FDs in R and hence from Inference 4.1.6 X$\rightarrow${A$_1$, ...A$_n$} is also a full FD. Thus from Lemma 5, X is a candidate key in Project(R, X $\cup$ {A$_1$, ...A$_n$}).

Let $Y{\rightarrow}B$ be a non trivial full functional dependency in Project(R, X $\cup$ {A_1, ...A_n}) where B is an informational attribute. We must prove that Y is a candidate key.

Since B is an informational attribute, it can't be part of the candidate key X and therefore B is in {A_1, ...A_n}. Further, $B = A_i$ for some i because B and each A_k consists of just one attribute. Thus $Y{\rightarrow}A_i$.

Case 1) All the attributes of Y are in X.

By the definition of minimal cover $X{\rightarrow}A_i$ is a full FD and since $Y{\rightarrow}A_i$ where Y is a subset of X, Y must equal X. As shown above, X is a candidate key in Project(R, X $\cup$ {A_1, ...A_n}) and thus so is Y.

Case 2) Some of the attributes of Y are in {A_1, ... A_n}. (We'll show that this case can't occur.)

Let Y' be those attributes of Y that aren't in X.

Without loss of generality, assume Y' = {A_1, ...A_m} for some m<i (where $Y{\rightarrow} A_i$).

Since $X{\rightarrow}A_1$, ... $X{\rightarrow}A_m$ we have from Inference 4.1.5 that $X{\rightarrow}${A_1, ...A_m}. By augmentation, $X{\rightarrow}X \cup$ {A_1, ...A_m}. Also, Since X $\cup$ {A_1, ...A_m} contains Y it follows that X $\cup$ {A_1, ...A_m}$\rightarrow A_i$. Hence, by augmentation and transitivity we can deduce that $X{\rightarrow}A_i$. Thus $X{\rightarrow}A_i$ can be constructed from the FDs $X{\rightarrow}A_1$, ... $X{\rightarrow}A_m$ and hence $X{\rightarrow}A_i$ can't be part of a minimal cover with $X{\rightarrow}A_1$, ... $X{\rightarrow}A_m$. Since this contradicts the assumptions, Case 2 isn't possible.

This completes the proof of Inference 5.3.7.

Theorem 5.3.8: Let {R_1, ...R_n} be the projections that form a decomposition of R resulting from the Dependency Preserving Decomposition Algorithm. Further, let C be a set of attributes that is a candidate key for R. Then {R_1, ...R_n, Project(R, C)} is a non loss, dependency preserving decomposition into 3NF.

Proof of Theorem 5.3.8: We omit this proof and refer the reader to reference [Ul] where a proof is presented using Algorithm 4.4.1 for determining if a decomposition is non loss.

Inference 5.3.9: Let R and {R_1, ...R_n} be the projections that form a decomposition of R resulting from the Dependency Preserving Decomposition Algorithm. If the attributes of any R_i are a super key for R, then {R_1, ...R_n} is a non loss, dependency preserving decomposition into 3NF.

Proof of Inference 5.3.9: Let the attributes of R_i be a super key for R where C is a subset of these attributes that's a candidate key. Then from Theorem 5.3.8, {R_1, ...R_n, Project(R, C)} is a non loss decomposition. Since Join is commutative and associative we can form R_i Join Project(R, C) as the first step in the join. of R_1, ...R_n, Project(R, C). Since R_i Join Project(R, C)=R_i, Project(R, C) is irrelevant in the join and {R_1, ...R_n} is non loss. From Theorem 5.3.6, {R_1, ...R_n} is also a dependency preserving decomposition in 3NF.

This completes the proof of Inference 5.3.9

We repeat the following definition for use in the four inferences that follow.

Boyce/Codd Normal Form (BCNF): A relation is in BCNF if and only if every determinant of an attribute in a non trivial full functional dependency is a candidate key.

Inference 5.4.1: A relation in BCNF is also in 3NF.

Proof of Inference 5.4.1: Assume that a relation, R, is in BCNF.

Recall that a relation is in 3NF if and only if every determinant of an informational attribute in a non trivial full functional dependency is a candidate key.

Let X be a set of attributes in R and Y be an informational attribute such that there is a non trivial full functional dependency $X{\rightarrow}Y$. We assume R is in BCNF, so X must be a candidate key and, by definition, R is in 3NF.

This completes the proof of Inference 5.4.1.

Inference 5.4.2: A relation is in BCNF if and only if every determinant of an attribute in a non trivial functional dependency is a super key.

Proof of Inference 5.4.2:

First, we'll assume that for some relation, R, every determinant of an attribute in a non trivial functional dependency is a super key and show that R is in BCNF. We must show that every determinant of an attribute in a non trivial full functional dependency is a candidate key.

Let $X \rightarrow Y$ be a non trivial full functional dependency where Y is an attribute. Then by assumption X is a super key. Let X' be a subset of X that's a candidate key. By Inference 4.1.3, $X' \rightarrow Y$. Since the functional dependency $X \rightarrow Y$ is full, X' can't be a proper subset of X and therefore X = X' and X is a candidate key.

Next, we'll assume that R is in BCNF and therefore every determinant of an attribute in a non trivial full functional dependency is a candidate key. We must show that every determinant of an attribute in a non trivial functional dependency is a super key.

Let R be a relation where X is a set of attributes and Y is an attribute such that there is a non trivial functional dependency $X \rightarrow Y$. Let X' be a subset of X such that $X' \rightarrow Y$ is a full functional dependency. Then by assumption X' is a candidate key and therefore X is a super key.

This completes the proof of Inference 5.4.2.

Inference 5.4.3: A relation is in BCNF if and only if every determinant in a non trivial functional dependency is a super key.

Proof of Inference 5.4.3:

First, we'll assume that for a relation, R, every determinant in a non trivial functional dependency is a super key and show that R is in BCNF. We must show that every determinant of an attribute in a non trivial full functional dependency is a candidate key.

Let R be a relation with a set of attributes, X, and an attribute, Y, such that there is a non trivial full functional dependency $X \rightarrow Y$. By assumption, X is a super key. Let X' be a subset of X that's a candidate key. Then, by Inference 4.1.3, $X' \rightarrow Y$. However, since $X \rightarrow Y$ is a full functional dependency, there's no proper subset of X on which Y is functionally dependent. Hence, X = X' and X is a candidate key.

Next, we'll assume that R is in BCNF; that is, every determinant of an attribute in a non trivial full functional dependency is a candidate key. We'll show that every determinant in a non trivial functional dependency is a super key.

Let R be a relation with sets of attributes, X and Y = {Y_1, Y_2, …Y_n} such that there is a non trivial functional dependency $X \rightarrow Y$. From Inference 4.1.5 we know that $X \rightarrow Y_i$ for each i from 1 to n. Since $X \rightarrow Y$ is non trivial, there is at least one attribute in Y, say Y_k, that isn't an attribute in X. Thus, $X \rightarrow Y_k$ is non trivial. Let X' be a subset of X such that $X' \rightarrow Y_k$ is a non trivial full functional dependency. Then, by assumption, X' is a candidate key and therefore X must be a super key.

This completes the proof of Inference 5.4.3.

Inference 5.4.4: If a relation is in 3NF and has no overlapping candidate keys, then it's also in BCNF.

Proof of Inference 5.4.4: Let R be a relation that's in 3NF with no overlapping candidate keys. To prove that R is in BCNF, we'll show that every determinant of an attribute in a non trivial full functional dependency is a candidate key. Let X be a set of attributes in R and Y be an attribute such that there is a non trivial full functional dependency $X \rightarrow Y$. We must show that X is a candidate key.

Case 1) Y is an informational attribute: By the definition of 3NF, every determinant of an informational attribute in a non trivial full functional dependency is a candidate key.

Case 2) Y is a candidate key: If Y is a candidate key, then it has a different value on every row of R and thus X – as a determinant of Y – must also have a different value on every row and, therefore, be a super key. Furthermore, if there is a proper subset of X, say X', that is a candidate key, then X'→Y. However, X→Y is a full functional dependency, so there is no proper subset of X such that X'→Y. Hence, X must be a candidate key.

Case 3) Y is not a candidate key but is part of one: Let Y' be a candidate key that contains the attribute Y.

Step 1. (Y'-Y) ∪ X is a super key.
Proof of Step 1: We'll show that the value of (Y'-Y) ∪ X is different on any two different rows. Let $(Y'-Y)_r$, X_r and $(Y'-Y)_s$, X_s be the values of (Y'-Y), X on rows r and s respectively.
If the value of (Y'-Y) ∪ X is the same on the two rows then $(Y'-Y)_r = (Y'-Y)_s$ and $X_r = X_s$. Since X→Y, $Y_r = Y_s$. However, if $(Y'-Y)_r = (Y'-Y)_s$ and $Y_r = Y_s$, then $Y'_r = Y'_s$. Because Y' is a candidate key it can't have the same value on two different rows. Thus, (Y'-Y) ∪ X must have different values on r and s and therefore (Y'-Y) ∪ X is a super key.

Step 2. X is a candidate key.
Proof of Step 2: From Step 1, (Y'-Y) ∪ X is a super key. Let C be a subset of (Y'-Y) ∪ X that is a candidate key. Note that since X→Y is nontrivial, Y isn't an attribute in X and thus not in (Y'-Y) ∪ X. Because C is a subset of (Y'-Y) ∪ X, Y isn't in C. Since Y is in Y', C and Y' are different candidate keys.
If X isn't a candidate key, then C ≠ X and C must contain at least one attribute, Y_c, in Y'-Y. Then Y_c is in C and in Y' and thus C and Y' are overlapping candidate keys. However, this is a contradiction because we assumed that there were no overlapping candidate keys. Thus, X must be a candidate key.

This completes the proof of Inference 5.4.4.

Inference 5.4.5: A relation is not in BCNF if there is an attribute, A, that's fully functionally dependent on a set of attributes, X, that isn't a candidate key and A isn't an attribute in X.

Proof of Inference 5.4.5:

Since A isn't an attribute in X, we have a determinant of an attribute in a non trivial, full functional dependency that isn't candidate key and thus the definition of BCNF is not met.

This completes the proof of Inference 5.4.5.

We repeat the following definition for use in the proofs of the two inferences that follow.

Fourth Normal Form (4NF): A Relation, R, is in 4NF if and only if whenever there exists subsets X, Y of the attributes of R such that there is a nontrivial MVD X→→Y, then X is a super key.

Inference 5.5.1: If R is a relation in 4NF, then every non trivial MVD is a non trivial FD whose determinant is a super key.

Proof of Inference 5.5.1: Let R be a relation in 4NF and let X, Y be subsets of the attributes of R such that there is a non trivial MVD X→→Y. We must show that X→Y is a non trivial FD.

Since R is in 4NF, by definition X is a super key. From Inference 4.1.3, every set of attributes in a relation is functionally dependent on every super key. Hence, there is an FD X→Y. Also, because X→→Y, it follows by definition that X and Y have no attributes in common and thus X→Y is a non trivial FD.

This completes the proof of Inference 5.5.1.

Inference 5.5.2: A relation in 4NF is also in BCNF and thus in all lower normal forms.

Proof of Inference 5.5.2:

Let R be a relation in 4NF where X is a subset of its attributes and Y is an attribute such that X→Y is a non-trivial full functional dependency. We'll show that X is a candidate key.

Case 1: All the attributes of R are in at least one of the attribute sets X, {Y}.
Then the X-values must be different on each row of R. For if the same X-value appeared on two different rows: The Y-values would also be the same, the two rows would be identical, and thus R wouldn't be a relation. Hence, X is a super key. Let X' be a subset of X that is a candidate key. Then we would have an FD X'→Y. However, since Y is fully functionally dependent on X, X' can't be a proper subset of X. Hence X = X' so X is a candidate key.
Case 2: There are attributes that are not in X and not in {Y}
Since X→Y is non-trivial, Y isn't an attribute in X and by Inference 4.2.3 there is an MVD X→→Y. From the assumption for Case 2, there are attributes that are not in X and not in {Y} and thus X→→Y is a non-trivial MVD. By assumption R is in 4NF and therefore X is a super key. Let X' be a subset of X that is a candidate key. Then we would have an X'→Y. However, since Y is fully functionally dependent on X, X' can't be a proper subset of X. Hence X is a candidate key.

This completes the proof of Inference 5.5.2

We repeat the following definition of Fifth Normal Form:
Fifth Normal Form (5NF): A Relation, R, is in 5NF if every JD in R is the result of candidate keys. That is, Algorithm 5.6.1 succeeds for R and every JD in R.

For convenience we repeat **Algorithm 5.6.1** for use in the proof of Inferences 5.6.2 and 5.6.3 that follow. Let $X_1, X_2, \ldots X_n$ be subsets of a relation R.

Step 1) Initialize a set, A, as $\{X_1, X_2, \ldots X_n\}$.
Step 2) If there is a candidate key in two of the attribute sets in A, replace these sets by their union.
Repeat Step 2 as long as there's some candidate key that's in two of the remaining attribute sets in A.

The algorithm is said to "succeed" for a relation R and the subsets of its attributes $X_1, X_2, \ldots X_n$ when the procedure terminates with a member of A containing all the attributes of R:

Inference 5.6.2: A relation in 5NF is also in 4NF and thus in all lower normal forms.

Proof of Inference 5.6.2:

Let R be a relation 5NF and let X and Y be subsets of the attributes of R such that there is a nontrivial MVD X→→Y. We must show that X is a super key.

Let Z be all the attributes in R that aren't in X or Y. We assume X→→Y so by Inference 4.4.6, R satisfies JD*(X ∪ Y, X ∪ Z). Since R is in 5NF, Algorithm 5.6.1 must succeed for R and JD*(X ∪ Y, X ∪ Z).
Step 1) Initialize A = {X ∪ Y, X ∪ Z}.
Because X→→Y is nontrivial, there's at least one attribute in Z and in Y. Since X, Y and Z have no attributes in common, neither X ∪ Y nor X ∪ Z contains all the attributes in R..
Step 2) For the algorithm to succeed there must be a candidate key in both X ∪ Y and X ∪ Z. Since X, Y and Z have no attributes in common, there must be a candidate key in X to make A = {X ∪ Y ∪ Z}.
Thus X contains a candidate key and is therefore a super key.

This completes the proof of Inference 5.6.2.

We now present the following Lemma to be used in the proof of Inference 5.6.3 that follows it.

Lemma 6: Let A and B be subsets of the attributes of a relation R that have a candidate key in common. Then Project(R, A) Join Project(R, B) = Project(R, A ∪ B).

Proof of Lemma 6: Let A have attribute names $A_1, \ldots A_n, C_1, \ldots C_m$ and B have attribute names $B_1, \ldots B_k$, $C_1, \ldots C_m$. We'll use a_i, b_i, and c_i to denote an attribute value for the attributes in A, B, and C respectively. The common attributes of A and B are $C_1, \ldots C_m$ and the heading of Project(R, A) Join Project(R, B) is A_1, $\ldots A_n, B_1, \ldots B_k, C_1, \ldots C_m$ that is the same as the heading for Project(R, A ∪ B).

The values $a_1, \ldots a_n, b_1, \ldots b_k, c_1, \ldots c_m$ form a row in the Project(R, A) Join Project(R, B) if and only if:

1) $a_1, \ldots a_n, c_1, \ldots c_m$ form a row in Project(R, A) AND 2) $b_1, \ldots b_k, c_1, \ldots c_m$ form a row in Project(R, B).

Let $a_1, \ldots a_n, b_1, \ldots b_k, c_1, \ldots c_m$ form a row in Project(R, A) Join Project(R, B). Then $a_1, \ldots a_n, c_1, \ldots c_m$ and $b_1, \ldots b_k, c_1, \ldots c_m$ form rows in Project(R, A) and Project(R, B) respectively. Hence $a_1, \ldots a_n, c_1, \ldots c_m$ and $b_1, \ldots b_k, c_1, \ldots c_m$ must each appear on a row in R. Since $\{c_1, \ldots c_m\}$ contains a candidate key, these values can only appear on a row together and thus $a_1, \ldots a_n, b_1, \ldots b_k, c_1, \ldots c_m$ are on a row in R and hence also form a row in Project(R, A ∪ B).

Conversely, if $a_1, \ldots a_n, b_1, \ldots b_k, c_1, \ldots c_m$ form a row in Project(R, A ∪ B), then 1) $a_1, \ldots a_n, c_1, \ldots c_m$ form a row in Project(R, A) and 2) $b_1, \ldots b_k, c_1, \ldots c_m$ form a row in Project(R, B). Thus $a_1, \ldots a_n, b_1, \ldots b_k, c_1, \ldots c_m$ is a row in Project(R, A) Join Project(R, B) thereby proving Lemma 6.

Inference 5.6.3: Let R be a relation and let $X_1, X_2, \ldots X_m$ be subsets of the attributes of R whose union was formed in the process of applying Algorithm 5.6.1. Then Project(R, $X_1 ∪ X_2 \ldots ∪ X_m$) = Project(R, X_1) JOIN Project(R, X_2)… JOIN Project(R, X_m).

Proof of Inference 5.6.3:

We'll prove this by using the method of "complete mathematical induction." First we'll show that the inference is true for m=2. Next, we'll show that if we assume that it's true for every integer less than some arbitrary integer m, it must be true for m. These two steps prove the inference is true for any value of m.

First, we'll prove that the inference is true for m=2:
Since $X_1 ∪ X_2$ was formed in applying Algorithm 5.6.1, X_1 and X_2 must have a candidate key in common. Hence, by Lemma 6, Project(R, X_1) JOIN Project(R, X_2) = Project(R, $X_1 ∪ X_2$) thereby proving that the inference is true for m=2.

Secondly, we'll show that if we assume the inference is true for all integers less than some arbitrary integer, m, it must also be true for m:

The last union done to obtain the union of $X_1, X_2, \ldots X_m$ involves the union of two sets that were each the result of less than m unions. Without loss of generality, we can assume that these two sets were the following unions: $(X_1 ∪ \ldots X_k)$ and $(X_{k+1} ∪ \ldots X_m)$ for some k less than m. Then these two unions both involve less than m subsets so by the complete induction assumption Project(R, $X_1 ∪ \ldots X_k$) = Project(R, X_1) Join Project(R, X_2)… Join Project(R, X_k) and Project(R, $X_{k+1} ∪ \ldots X_m$) = Project(R, X_{k+1}) Join Project(R, X_2)… Join Project(R, X_m).

Therefore Project(R, X_1) Join Project(R, X_2)… Project(R, X_k) Join Project(R, X_{k+1}) Join Project(R, X_m) = Project(R, $X_1 ∪ \ldots X_k$) Join Project(R, $X_{k+1} ∪ \ldots X_m$). Since $X_1 ∪ \ldots X_k$ and $X_{k+1} ∪ \ldots X_m$ must have a candidate key in common, it follows from Lemma 6 that Project(R, $X_1 ∪ \ldots X_k$) Join Project(R, $X_{k+1} ∪ \ldots X_m$)= Project(R, $X_1 ∪ \ldots X_m$). Thus we have shown that Project(R, $X_1 ∪ \ldots X_m$) = Project(R, X_1) Join Project(R, X_2)… Join Project(R, X_m).

This completes the proof of Inference 5.6.3.

Inference 5.6.4: Let R be a relation and $X_1, X_2, \ldots X_n$ be subsets of the attributes of R for which Algorithm 5.6.1.succeeds. Then the projections of R on $X_1, X_2, \ldots X_n$ form a non-loss decomposition of R.

Proof of Inference 5.6.4:

Let R be a relation and $X_1, X_2, \ldots X_n$ be subsets of the attributes of R for which Algorithm 5.6.1.succeeds. We must show that R = Project(R, X_1) Join Project(R, X_2)… Join Project(R, X_n).

Since R and $\{X_1, X_2, \ldots X_n\}$ satisfy Algorithm 5.6.1, there must be m of the subsets of attributes – for some $m \leq n$ – whose union results from the algorithm and contains all the attributes in R. Without loss of generality, we can assume that these subsets are $X_1, X_2, \ldots X_m$.

From Inference 5.6.3 we have Project(R, $X_1 \cup \ldots X_m$) = Project(R, X_1) Join Project(R, X_2)… Join Project(R, X_m). Since $X_1 \cup \ldots X_m$ has all the attributes of R, Project(R, $X_1 \cup \ldots X_m$) = R. Therefore R = Project(R, X_1) Join Project(R, X_2)… Join Project(R, X_m). We can then express Project(R, X_1) Join Project(R, X_2)… Project(R, X_m) Join Project(R, X_{m+1})… Join Project(R, X_n) as R Join (Project(R, X_{m+1}) … Join Project(R, X_n)).

We must show that R = R Join (Project(R, X_{m+1}) … Join Project(R, X_n)). By the "General Definition of Join" given in Chapter 3, the result of these joins has attributes $A_1, A_2, \ldots A_k$ and consists of all the rows (a_1, $a_2, \ldots a_k$) where:

1) Every attribute A_i appears in at least one of R, Project(R, X_{m+1}), … Project(R, X_n).
2) The values in $\{a_1, a_2, \ldots a_k\}$ corresponding to the attributes of R form a row in R and the values corresponding to $X_{m+1}, \ldots X_n$ form rows in Project(R, X_{m+1}), … Project(R, X_n), respectively.

It follows from 1) above that that $A_1, A_2, \ldots A_k$ are the attributes in R.

First, assume that ($a_1, a_2, \ldots a_k$) is a row in R. Then it satisfies 2) above and therefore it's also a row in R Join (Project(R, X_{m+1}) … Join Project(R, X_n)).

Next, assume that ($a_1, a_2, \ldots a_k$) is a row in R Join (Project(R, X_{m+1}) … Join Project(R, X_n)). Because $A_1, A_2, \ldots A_k$ are the attributes in R, the values of $\{a_1, a_2, \ldots a_k\}$ corresponding to the attributes of R equal ($a_1, a_2, \ldots a_k$). Hence, to satisfy 2 above ($a_1, a_2, \ldots a_k$) must be a row in R.

Thus R = R Join (Project(R, X_{m+1}) … Join Project(R, X_n)) and from above we have R = Project(R, X_1) Join Project(R, X_2)… Join Project(R, X_m). Hence R = Project(R, X_1) Join Project(R, X_2) … Join Project(R, X_n).

This completes the proof for Inference 5.6.4

Inference 5.6.5: For a relation R in 5NF, the addition or deletion of a row will never cause the violation of a join dependency in R. That is, for any JD*($X_1, X_2, \ldots X_n$), R will still be equal to the join of its projections on $X_1, X_2 \ldots X_n$ after a row is added to or deleted from R.

Proof of Inference 5.6.5:

Since by assumption R is in 5NF, Algorithm 5.6.1 succeeds for R and the JD*($X_1, X_2, \ldots X_n$). By Inference 5.6.4, R = Project(R, X_1) Join Project(R, X_2)… Join Project(R, X_n).

This completes the proof of Inference 5.6.5.

This concludes the Appendix.

References

[ABU]   A. V. Aho, C. Beeri and J. D. Ullman. "The Theory of Joins in Relational Databases." ACM Transactions on Database Systems, Vol. 4, No. 3, September 1979, Pages 297-314.

[Da1]   C. J. Date. "An Introduction to Database Systems (6th edition)." Addison–Wesley (1995).

[Da2]   C. J. Date. "The Outer Join." in *Relational Database: Selected Writings*. Addison-Wesley (1986).

[Da3]   C. J. Date. "Simple Conditions for Guaranteeing Higher Normal Forms in Relational Databases." in *Relational Database Writings 1989-1991*. Addison-Wesley (1992).

[Fa1]   Ronald Fagin "Multivalued Dependencies and a New Normal Form for Relational Dependencies" ACM Transactions on Database Systems, Vol. 2, No. 3, September 1977, Pages 262-278.

[Fa2]   Ronald Fagin. "Normal Forms and Relational Database Operators" Proceedings of the 1979 ACM SIGMOD International Conference on Management of Data, Boston Mass. PP 153-160.

[Ri]   Jorma Rissanen. "Independent Components of Relations." ACM Transactions on Database Systems, Vol. 2, No. 4, December 1977. Page 317-325.

[Ul]   Jeffrey D. Ullman. "Principles of Database and Knowledge–Base Systems Volume I." Computer Science Press, Inc.

[Wa]   Andrew Warden (Hugh Darwen). "Adventures in Relationland." in *Relational Database Writings 1985-1989*. Addison-Wesley (1990).

INDEX